Pediatric Pharmacology

1st Edition

By
Rosmarie Fuller, RNC, MSN, NNP, PNP-CS, IBCLC

21 Bristol Drive
South Easton, MA 02375
1-800-618-1670

ABOUT THE AUTHOR

Rosmarie Fuller RNC, MSN, NNP, PNP-CS, IBCLC, graduated from Northeastern University in Boston in 1974 with a BSN, and she received her MSN from the University of Chicago in 1982. She completed certification as a Neonatal Nurse Practitioner in 1991. In 2000, she completed a post-master's certificate program as a Pediatric Nurse Practitioner (PNP) at Regis College in Weston, Massachusetts. Ms. Fuller has worked for 28 years in the field of neonatology as a staff nurse, childbirth educator, CPR instructor, neonatal nurse practitioner, clinical specialist, lactation consultant, and clinical educator. She has also worked for the past five years in a graduate nursing program as clinical faculty and staff PNP and is currently employed as a PNP part time in private practice. She has published several articles and CEU programs, has lectured on both neonatal and pediatric topics, and maintains certifications as an NNP, PNP, lactation consultant, Neonatal Resuscitation Program (NRP) instructor, Pediatric Advanced Life Support provider, and Perinatal Continuing Education Program (PCEPs) instructor.

ABOUT THE SUBJECT MATTER EXPERT

Colleen Marie Quinn, RN, MSN, graduated from Trocaire College in Buffalo, New York with an Associate Degree in Nursing in 1977 and later went on to graduate from Southern Illinois University with a Bachelor's Degree in Psychology. Most recently, she earned her Master's degree in Nursing from Florida Atlantic University in Boca Raton, Florida. Ms. Quinn's working career, now going on 26 years, includes geriatric nursing, neonatology, and pediatrics. Colleen is currently employed as a full-time assistant professor of nursing at Broward Community College in Pembroke Pines, Florida where she teaches Pediatrics and Math for Nurses. She has published material related to nursing and cognitive development in children.

Copy Editor: Demi Rasmussen

Indexer: Sylvia Coates

Typesetter: Kathy Johnson

Western Schools' courses are designed to provide nursing professionals with the educational information they need to enhance their career development. The information provided within these course materials is the result of research and consultation with prominent nursing and medical authorities and is, to the best of our knowledge, current and accurate. However, the courses and course materials are provided with the understanding that Western Schools is not engaged in offering legal, nursing, medical, or other professional advice.

Western Schools' courses and course materials are not meant to act as a substitute for seeking out professional advice or conducting individual research. When the information provided in the courses and course materials is applied to individual circumstances, all recommendations must be considered in light of the uniqueness pertaining to each situation.

Western Schools' course materials are intended solely for *your* use and *not* for the benefit of providing advice or recommendations to third parties. Western Schools devoids itself of any responsibility for adverse consequences resulting from the failure to seek nursing, medical, or other professional advice. Western Schools further devoids itself of any responsibility for updating or revising any programs or publications presented, published, distributed, or sponsored by Western Schools unless otherwise agreed to as part of an individual purchase contract.

ISBN: 1-57801-081-0

COPYRIGHT© 2003—Western Schools, Inc. All Rights Reserved. No part(s) of this material may be reprinted, reproduced, transmitted, stored in a retrieval system, or otherwise utilized, in any form or by any means electronic or mechanical, including photocopying or recording, now existing or hereinafter invented, nor may any part of this course be used for teaching without the written permission from the publisher and author.

FPO303SH

IMPORTANT: Read these instructions *BEFORE* proceeding!

Enclosed with your course book you will find the FasTrax® answer sheet. Use this form to answer all the final exam questions that appear in this course book. If you are completing more than one course, be sure to write your answers on the appropriate answer sheet. Full instructions and complete grading details are printed on the FasTrax instruction sheet, also enclosed with your order. Please review them before starting. *If you are mailing your answer sheet(s) to Western Schools, we recommend you make a copy as a backup.*

ABOUT THIS COURSE

A "Pretest" is provided with each course to test your current knowledge base regarding the subject matter contained within this course. Your "Final Exam" is a multiple choice examination. **You will find the exam questions at the end of each chapter.** Some smaller hour courses include the exam at the end of the book.

In the event the course has less than 100 questions, mark your answers to the questions in the course book and leave the remaining answer boxes on the FasTrax answer sheet blank. **Use a black pen to fill in your answer sheet.**

A PASSING SCORE

You must score 70% or better in order to pass this course and receive your Certificate of Completion. Should you fail to achieve the required score, we will send you an additional FasTrax answer sheet so that you may make a second attempt to pass the course. Western Schools will allow you three chances to pass the same course…*at no extra charge!* After three failed attempts to pass the same course, your file will be closed.

RECORDING YOUR HOURS

Please monitor the time it takes to complete this course using the handy log sheet on the other side of this page. See below for transferring study hours to the course evaluation.

COURSE EVALUATIONS

In this course book you will find a short evaluation about the course you are soon to complete. This information is vital to providing the school with feedback on this course. The course evaluation answer section is in the lower right hand corner of the FasTrax answer sheet marked "Evaluation" with answers marked 1–25. Your answers are important to us, please take five minutes to complete the evaluation.

On the back of the FasTrax instruction sheet there is additional space to make any comments about the course, the school, and suggested new curriculum. Please mail the FasTrax instruction sheet, with your comments, back to Western Schools in the envelope provided with your course order.

TRANSFERRING STUDY TIME

Upon completion of the course, transfer the total study time from your log sheet to question #25 in the Course Evaluation. The answers will be in ranges, please choose the proper hour range that best represents your study time. You MUST log your study time under question #25 on the course evaluation.

EXTENSIONS

You have 2 years from the date of enrollment to complete this course. A six (6) month extension may be purchased. If after 30 months from the original enrollment date you do not complete the course, *your file will be closed and no certificate can be issued.*

CHANGE OF ADDRESS?

In the event you have moved during the completion of this course please call our student services department at 1-800-618-1670 and we will update your file.

A GUARANTEE TO WHICH YOU'LL GIVE HIGH HONORS

If any continuing education course fails to meet your expectations or if you are not satisfied in any manner, for any reason, you may return it for an exchange or a refund (less shipping and handling) within 30 days. Software, video and audio courses must be returned unopened.

Thank you for enrolling at Western Schools!

WESTERN SCHOOLS
P.O. Box 1930
Brockton, MA 02303
(800) 618-1670

Pediatric Pharmacology

P.O. Box 1930
Brockton, MA 02303

Please use this log to total the number of hours you spend reading the text and taking the final examination (use 50-min hours).

Date	Hours Spent
_____	_____
_____	_____
_____	_____
_____	_____
_____	_____
_____	_____
_____	_____
_____	_____
_____	_____
_____	_____
_____	_____
_____	_____
_____	_____
	TOTAL [ ]

Please log your study hours with submission of your final exam. To log your study time, fill in the appropriate circle under question 25 of the FasTrax® answer sheet under the "Evaluation" section.

PLEASE LOG YOUR STUDY HOURS WITH SUBMISSION OF YOUR FINAL EXAM. Please choose the answer that represents the total study hours it took you to complete this 10 hour course.

A. less than 5 hours

B. 5–8 hours

C. 9–12 hours

D. greater than 12 hours

Pediatric Pharmacology

WESTERN SCHOOLS
CONTINUING EDUCATION EVALUATION

Instructions: Mark your answers to the following questions with a black pen on the "Evaluation" section of your FasTrax® answer sheet provided with this course. You should not return this sheet. Please use the scale below to rate the following statements:

    A Agree Strongly   C Disagree Somewhat
    B Agree Somewhat   D Disagree Strongly

The course content met the following education objectives

1. Identified the principles of pharmacodynamics and pharmacotherapeutics and indicated the impact of physiological differences between the very young and the older child on drug administration.

2. Specified the classifications of cardio-respiratory medications and indicated the applicable nursing implications for the administration of these drugs.

3. Specified the classifications of gastrointestinal and genitourinary medications and indicated the applicable nursing implications for the administration of these drugs.

4. Specified the classifications of vaccines and antibiotic medications and indicated the applicable nursing implications for the administration of these drugs.

5. Specified the classifications of neurological and pain medications and indicated the applicable nursing implications for the administration of these drugs.

6. Specified the classifications of dermatological medications and indicated the applicable nursing implications for the administration of these drugs.

7. This offering met my professional education needs.

8. The objectives met the overall purpose/goal of the course.

9. The course was generally well written and the subject matter explained thoroughly. (If no please explain on the back of the FasTrax instruction sheet.)

10. The content of this course was appropriate for home study.

11. The final examination was well written and at an appropriate level for the content of the course.

Please complete the following research questions in order to help us better meet your educational needs. Pick the ONE answer which is most appropriate.

12. Why do you choose home study to fulfill some or all of your license renewal requirements?
    A. Price
    B. Convenience to study when you want
    C. Permanent reference material
    D. Large variety of course selections

13. Why did you select Western Schools as your Continuing Education provider?
    A. Broad list of professional accreditations
    B. Service/Delivery
    C. Reputation for quality, up-to-date course materials
    D. Price

14. How did you fulfill the majority of your CE requirement the time just before this Western Schools order?
    A. Western Schools
    B. Another home study provider
    C. Seminars or in-house lectures
    D. No previous occasion

15. Which answer best describes the portion of your total Continuing Education hours that were completed by home study during your last renewal?
    A. All
    B. Half to more than half
    C. Less than half
    D. None

16. Are you reimbursed for your Continuing Education hours, and if so, by what dollar percentage?
    A. All
    B. Half to more than half
    C. Less than half
    D. None

17. What is your work status?
    A. Full-time employment
    B. Part-time employment
    C. Per diem/Temporary employment
    D. Inactive/Retired

18. For your LAST renewal did you take more Continuing Education contact hours than required by your state, if so, how many?
    A. 1–15 hours
    B. 16–30 hours
    C. 31 or more hours
    D. No, I only take the state required minimum

19. Do you usually exceed the contact hours required for your state license renewal, and if so, why?
    A. Yes, I have more than one state license
    B. Yes, to meet additional special association Continuing Education requirements
    C. Yes, for professional self-interest/cross-training
    D. No, I only take the state required minimum

20. What nursing shift do you most commonly work?
    A. Morning Shift (Any shift starting after 3:00am or before 11:00am)
    B. Day/Afternoon Shift (Any shift starting after 11:00am or before 7:00pm)
    C. Night Shift (Any shift starting after 7:00pm or before 3:00am)
    D. I work rotating shifts

21. What was the SINGLE most important reason you chose this course?
    A. Low price
    B. New or newly revised course
    C. High interest/Required course topic
    D. Number of contact hours needed

22. Where do you work? (If your place of employment is not listed below, please leave this question blank.)
    A. Hospital
    B. Medical clinic/Group practice/HMO/Office setting
    C. Long term care/Rehabilitation facility/Nursing home
    D. Home health care agency

23. Which field do you specialize in?
    A. Medical/Surgical
    B. Geriatrics
    C. Pediatrics/Neonatal
    D. Other

24. For your last renewal, how many months BEFORE your license expiration date did you order your course materials?
    A. 1–3 months
    B. 4–6 months
    C. 7–12 months
    D. Greater than 12 months

25. **PLEASE LOG YOUR STUDY HOURS WITH SUBMISSION OF YOUR FINAL EXAM.** Please choose which best represents the total study hours it took to complete this 10 hour course.
    A. less than 5 hours
    B. 5–8 hours
    C. 9–12 hours
    D. greater than 12 hours

CONTENTS

Pretest xi
Introduction xiii
Chapter 1 **Principles of Pharmacology** 1
    Pharmacodynamics, Pharmacokinetics, and Receptor Sites 1
    Administration and Absorption 2
    Protein Binding 3
    Distribution 4
    Metabolism 4
    Elimination 4
    Monitoring Drug Levels 5
    Exam Questions 7
Chapter 2 **Cardio-Respiratory Drugs** 9
    Anti-Arrhythmics 9
        Class 1 - Sodium Channel Blockers 10
        Class 2 - Beta Blockers 10
        Class 3 - Potassium Channel Blockers 11
        Class 4 - Calcium Channel Blockers 11
        Miscellaneous Anti-Arrhythmics 11
    Anti-Hypertensives 12
        Centrally Acting Nervous System Agents 12
        Peripheral-Acting CNS Agents 13
        Angiotensin Converting Enzyme (ACE) Inhibitors 13
    Reactive Airway Disease 13
        Short-Acting Beta 2 Agonists 14
        Long-Acting Beta 2 Agonists 15
        Inhaled Corticosteroids 15
        Mast Cell Stabilizers 16
        Anticholinergics 16
        Leukotriene Modifiers 17
    Allergies 17
        Decongestants 17
        Antihistamines 18
        Antitussives 18
    Exam Questions 21

Chapter 3 Genitourinary, Gastrointestinal and Endocrine Medications 23

    Diuretics 23

        Thiazide Diuretics 23

        Loop Diuretics 24

        Potassium-Sparing Diuretics 24

        Carbonic Anhydrase Inhibitors 25

        Osmotic Diuretics 25

    Primary Nocturnal Enuresis 26

    Gastroesophageal Reflux 26

        Antacids 27

        H2 Antagonists 27

        Proton Pump Inhibitors 28

        Prokinetics 28

    Nutritional Supplements 29

    Diabetic Medications 29

    Thyroid Medications 31

        Thyroid Supplementation 31

        Antithyroid Drugs 31

    Exam Questions 33

Chapter 4 Antibiotics and Vaccines 35

    The Immune Response 35

    Vaccines 37

        General Vaccination Considerations 37

        General Contraindications 38

        Vaccination is not Contraindicated in 38

    Antibiotics 41

        Folate Antagonists/Inhibitors of Folate Reduction 41

        Drugs That Inhibit Cell Wall Synthesis 42

        Drugs That Inhibit Protein Synthesis 43

        Drugs That Inhibit Nucleic Acid Function 43

    Exam Questions 45

Chapter 5 Neurological Medications 47

    Pain Medications 47

        NSAIDS 48

        Non-Narcotic Analgesics 48

        Narcotics/Opiates 49

    Headache 50

        Ergotamine 50

Table of Contents–
Pediatric Pharmacology

    Psychiatric Drugs 51
        Selective Serotonin Reuptake Inhibitors (SSRI) 51
        Tricyclic Antidepressants (TCAs) 52
        Monoamine Oxidase Inhibitors (MAOIs) 52
        Miscellaneous and Newer Antidepressants 52
        Antianxiolytics 53
    Attention Deficit Hyperactivity Disorder (ADHD) 54
        Stimulants 54
        Antidepressants 55
        Antihypertensives 55
    Seizure Medications 55
    Ophthalmologic Medications 58
    Exam Questions 59

Chapter 6 **Dermatological Medications** 61
    Skin Lesions 61
    Exam Questions 65

Appendix 1 **Summary of Drug Interactions** 67
Appendix 2 **Summary of Factors Affecting Drug Therapy in the Very Young Child** 69
Appendix 3 **Calculating Dosages** 71
Appendix 4 **Resuscitation Medications** 73
Appendix 5 **Pregnancy Risk Categories** 75
Appendix 6 **Intraosseous Infusion** 77
Glossary 79
Bibliography 83
Index 85
Pretest Key 90

PRETEST

Begin by taking the pretest. Compare your answers on the pretest to the answer key (located in the back of the book). Circle those test items that you missed. The pretest answer key indicates the course chapters where the content of that question is discussed. Circle the answers to the pretest questions. Do not log pretest questions on the Faxtrax answer sheet.

Next, read each chapter. Focus special attention on the chapters where you made incorrect answer choices. Exam questions are provided at the end of each chapter so that you can assess your progress and understanding of the material.

1. Distribution of a medication is defined as
   a. dissemination of the drug throughout the body.
   b. dissemination of the drug from the circulation to the desired site of action.
   c. movement of the drug into the hepatic circulation.
   d. movement of the drug into the circulation.

2. One physiologic factor which affects the required dosage of a drug is
   a. volume of distribution.
   b. pinocytosis.
   c. active diffusion.
   d. the blood brain barrier.

3. An arrhythmia which arises from above the bundle of HIS is called
   a. ventricular tachycardia.
   b. supraventricular tachycardia.
   c. premature ventricular contractions.
   d. ventricular fibrillation.

4. The most effective way to administer inhaled medications to a child under the age of five years is
   a. to substitute a non-inhaled medication.
   b. a nebulizer with a mask.
   c. an MDI with powdered medication only.
   d. an MDI with a spacer.

5. The drug of choice in primary nocturnal enuresis is
   a. desmopressin.
   b. ergotamine.
   c. spironalactone.
   d. furosemide.

6. The type of medication which induces active immunity is
   a. attenuated vaccine.
   b. immunoglobulin.
   c. antibiotic.
   d. fibronectin.

7. A pain medication which is useful in fever, pain, and inflammation is

   a. acetominophen.
   b. ibuprofen.
   c. morphine.
   d. naloxone.

8. The safest class of antidepressant medication to administer to children is

   a. selective serotonin reuptake inhibitors.
   b. monoamine oxidase inhibitors.
   c. tricyclic antidepressants.
   d. antipsychotics.

9. The underlying pathophysiology behind attention deficit disorder is

   a. insufficient circulating norepinephrine.
   b. excessive circulating epinephrine.
   c. imbalance of dopamine and serotonin.
   d. insufficient circulating epinephrine.

10. The drug of choice in pediculosis (lice) is

    a. mupirocin.
    b. mebendazole.
    c. permethrin.
    d. clotrimazole.

INTRODUCTION

DISCLAIMER

Only about thirty percent of medications currently available have been FDA approved for use in the pediatric population. In 1997, the FDA Modernization Act was signed into law, which encourages drug companies to conduct pediatric drug studies by allowing or extending market exclusivity of drugs designated under the Act. This Act, plus the required expansion of the pediatric section of drug inserts for prescription drugs, will assist in disseminating information and safety considerations in pediatric drug therapy (Skidmore-Roth, 2003).

Our knowledge of pharmacology is constantly growing through clinical experience and research. Great care has been taken in this manuscript to ensure the accuracy and timeliness of the information presented, incorporating up-to-date, evidence-based practice. However, the author cannot be responsible for the continuing currency of the information presented or for any consequences which arise from clinical application of this information.

In addition, the drug listings include action, indications, contraindications, and side effects based on the pediatric patient. However, because of the variations between formulations, differences between trade and generic drugs, and the wide range of ages and weights upon which many drug dosages are based, doses will not be included in the listings. Readers are referred to the reference list and texts of their choice for dosing. Side effects listed in normal font are common side effects; those listed in bold font are serious or life-threatening.

INTRODUCTION

The goal of drug therapy in the pediatric patient is to safely administer a medication with a predictable effect to treat or prevent a medical condition. Although our knowledge of pediatric physiology is extensive, we still do not understand entirely the physiologic effects of drugs in this population. The incidence of adverse drug effects and medication errors is increasing, becoming a significant cause of morbidity and mortality in the adult as well as the pediatric patient. This course reviews information important for nurses to have when administering or prescribing medications to pediatric patients. The pharmacodynamics and pharmacokinetics are discussed to build understanding of the pharmacology of the most common medications used in this population of patients. The medications are presented by systems with a focus on the pathophysiology of common illnesses. Each class of drugs presented includes a representative list of drugs. An exhaustive description of each drug is beyond the scope of this manuscript, however, so only the most commonly prescribed drug-in-class will be spotlighted. The appendices cover such topics as resuscitation medications, drug calculations, a summary of physiologic factors which impact on drug administration, classifications of drugs used in pregnancy, and one method of interosseous infusion.

NOTE: The references for the listing of drugs-in-class are: the *Pediatric Drug Dosage Handbook* (Takemoto, Hodding & Kraus, 2001–2002), *Mosby's Nursing Drug Reference* (Skidmore-Roth, 2003), and the *Harriet Lane Handbook* (Gunn &

Nechyba, 2002). Further reference will not be made after each drug.

COURSE GOAL

After completion of this program, the reader will be conversant in pediatric pharmacotherapy and should be able to describe the physiologic basis for the administration of common medications as well as the nursing implications of medication therapy in the pediatric patient.

CHAPTER 1

PRINCIPLES OF PHARMACOLOGY

CHAPTER OBJECTIVE

After completing this chapter, the reader will be able to identify the principles of pharmacodynamics and pharmacotherapeutics and to indicate the impact of physiological differences between the very young and the older child on drug administration.

LEARNING OBJECTIVES

At the completion of the chapter, the reader will be able to

1. indicate the ways in which medications are administered, absorbed, distributed, metabolized, and eliminated from the body.
2. specify the significance of receptor sites.
3. identify key concepts in drug level monitoring.

PHARMACODYNAMICS, PHARMACOKINETICS, AND RECEPTOR SITES

An understanding of the effects of drug therapy requires knowledge of pharmacodynamics and pharmacokinetics. Pharmacodynamics is defined as the physiologic effect drugs have in the body and their mechanism of action. The intrinsic action of a drug is exerted when it binds with a receptor site on the target organ or site of action, producing a nerve impulse that then generates a biological response. The amount of drug required to stimulate a biological response is its *potency*; the maximum response a drug is able to produce is described as its *efficacy*.

The central nervous system, divided into the *autonomic* component and the *parasympathetic* component, produces nerve impulses through the use of neurotransmitters; that is, chemicals capable of transmitting an impulse across a neuromuscular junction. Receptor sites in the autonomic system are called adrenergic sites because they respond to the neurotransmitter epinephrine, also known as adrenaline. The autonomic nervous system produces a "fight or flight" response when stimulated. The parasympathetic receptor sites are called cholinergic receptors because the transmitter utilized is acetylcholine. The parasympathetic nervous system produces a "rest and digest" response.

At a site of action, drugs may stimulate a purely adrenergic or cholinergic response or a combination of the two, depending on the type of receptors present in the target site. Drugs are further classified as either *agonists*, those drugs that directly stimulate a receptor site, or *antagonists*, which inhibit the response of the receptor site. Cholinergic agonists produce a classic cholinergic response that includes increased secretions (tears, pulmonary secretions, and salivation), increased GI motility and tone, bladder relaxation, decreased heart rate, and decreased myocardial contractility.

An example of a cholinergic agonist is bethanechol (Urecholine®), which is used to treat urinary retention. Cholinergic antagonists block the cholinergic response and produce dry mouth, blurred vision, and increased heart rate. Examples of these types of drugs are atropine, used preoperatively, ipratropium (Atrovent®), a drug used in respiratory illness, and scopolamine (Hyoscine®).

In the same way, the autonomic nervous system has four types of receptor sites that, when stimulated, produce different effects. These sites are:

Alpha 1 (a1) sites - when stimulated by an agonist, produce vasoconstriction, increased peripheral resistance, increased blood pressure, and increased tone in the bladder sphincter.

Alpha 2 (a2) sites - when stimulated, inhibit the release of norepinephrine and insulin.

Beta 1 (b1) sites - stimulation increases heart rate, myocardial contractility, and increased lipolysis.

Beta 2 (b2) sites - stimulation produces vasodilation, bronchodilation, decreased peripheral vascular resistance, increased glycogenolysis, release of glucagon, and relaxation of the bladder sphincter and uterine smooth muscle.

Knowledge of the actions of direct stimulation and inhibition of these receptor sites is key to understanding how drugs work and how they may interact. For example, the effects of a short-acting beta agonist, such as albuterol, are negated when combined with a beta blocker, such as atenolol, a drug used in the management of hypertension (Harvey & Champe, 1997).

ADMINISTRATION AND ABSORPTION

In order to be effective, a drug must be administered in a dose and by a route that will enable it to reach a therapeutic level at the site of action. Our current understanding of qualitative and quantitative differences in physiologic functioning between children and adults has resulted in dose calculations that take into consideration weight and gestational age as well as the body composition of the pediatric patient.

The timing of dose administration affects serum concentration. Drugs given in a single dose reach a peak level that will gradually return to zero. Multiple doses of a drug given without an initial loading dose will attain peak and trough levels, within which a therapeutic level is achieved. The time required to reach the therapeutic range may be several half-lives of the drug. Administration of a loading dose decreases the amount of time required for the drug to reach a steady therapeutic range. A constant infusion is required for drugs with particularly short half-lives; this type of administration results in rapid achievement of a therapeutic level with minimum fluctuation between peak and trough levels.

Absorption describes movement of the drug into the circulation after administration and is affected by route, molecular weight, lipid solubility, and membrane transport characteristics. Membrane transport occurs by several mechanisms:

- *passive diffusion* - a drug moves from an area of greater to lesser concentration.
- *active diffusion* - a drug is bound to a carrier molecule and carried across the membrane; this process requires additional energy.
- *facilitated diffusion* - a drug is bound to a carrier molecule and "rides" across the membrane. This process does not require extra energy.
- *pinocytosis* - the drug molecule is engulfed by a cell membrane and incorporated into the cell.
- *pore transport* - the drug molecule passes through openings in the cell membrane.

In pediatric patients, most drugs are administered through the intravenous, subcutaneous, intramuscular, or enteral routes. Other routes of administration include inhalation, topical, intrathecal (into the subarachnoid space of the spinal cord), or intraventricular (directly into the ventricles of the brain). Absorption through the *intravenous* route is instantaneous and provides rapid, reliable, and predictable distribution of the drug throughout the intravascular compartment. There are potential problems with this method, however. Maintaining intravenous access is a concern, particularly with long-term therapy. Uneven or delayed delivery of the drug may be caused by retrograde administration; that is, administration of the drug into the tubing away from the patient. The rate of flow, adherence of the drug to the tubing lumen, or frequency of tubing changes may result in unpredictable or variable absorption. Because the drug is immediately distributed to the intravascular space, the risk of adverse affects is a real one. Therefore, drugs administered intravenously should be infused through a port as near to the patient as possible.

The absorption of a drug administered *intramuscularly* depends on muscle perfusion and circulation. In pediatric patients, these elements can be drastically altered by such conditions as shock, hypothermia, sepsis, hypoglycemia, and acidosis. When a drug is administered intramuscularly and is not completely absorbed, it accumulates into pockets and is unevenly released, resulting in unpredictable serum concentration.

A further risk of intramuscular, as well as intravenous, drug administration is the risk of "dead space overdose." There is a small amount of dead space in the hub of syringes, which may amount to 0.1–0.2 cc of fluid. When a medication is drawn up in a syringe, followed by the diluent in the same syringe, the additional medication in the hub is mixed with the diluent, so the amount of drug administered can exceed the required dose. To avoid this problem, it may be helpful to draw up the medication and diluent separately, then combine the two.

The absorption of drugs administered *orally (or enterally)* is affected by lipid or fat solubility of the drug, intestinal surface area available for absorption, gastric emptying time, and gastrointestinal perfusion. Not all of an enterally administered drug may reach the circulation. The amount of enterally administered drug that is absorbed into the circulation is termed the *bioavailability* of the drug.

Delivery of *inhaled* medications to sites of action in the lung depends on characteristics of the airways, ventilation pattern, and particle size of the inhalant. In the smaller airways of very young children, uneven ventilation perfusion pattern and increased secretion of mucous affect the degree of penetration of inhaled drugs.

Topically administered drugs may be absorbed at an unpredictable rate. The skin of younger children is characterized by decreased elastin and collagen fibers, increased fluid content, increased permeability and fragility, and higher pH. These characteristics increase the risks of mechanical and chemical injury as well as variable absorption.

Although drugs given intravenously may not reach adequate levels in the central nervous system due to the blood-brain barrier, this method of administration is preferred when using a medication that has adequate CNS penetration, since the intrathecal and intraventricular routes have been found to be unreliable and potentially dangerous (Starr, 2000).

PROTEIN BINDING

The amount of drug that is bound to protein will affect the required dose of that drug, since the bound fraction is *inactive*. Protein molecules are larger in general than are most drug molecules, so one protein molecule may bind and inactivate several molecules of a given drug. Very young children have less plasma protein compared with older children as well as decreased affinity for protein binding, which will affect the required dose.

DISTRIBUTION

Distribution of a drug describes the dissemination of the drug from the circulation to the site of action. The drug is first transported through the circulation to areas of high perfusion, such as the heart, lungs, liver, and kidneys, and more slowly to areas of lesser perfusion, such as the skin, muscles, and fat. Once absorbed, the drug is distributed directly through the extracellular fluid compartment (ECF) to the site of action. The drug may also be distributed through the ECF to a peripheral site of action, as in the administration of an antibiotic to treat meningitis or a localized infection. An understanding of these processes is important in calculating drug dosages. The volume of the ECF, affected by hydration status, is helpful in estimating the volume of body fluid and tissue the drug will eventually enter. This volume is called the volume of distribution (Vd) and varies among pediatric patients, being determined by the amount of body water and fat. A water-soluble drug has a larger volume of distribution in a very young child because of the greater percentage of body water. Similarly, fat-soluble drugs have a larger volume of distribution in older pediatric patients due to the greater amount of fat tissue in these patients. Drug level monitoring is based in part on the concept of volume of distribution; many drug manuals provide this information to assist in dose calculation.

METABOLISM

The P-450 enzyme system is a group of enzymes found in the liver that is involved in metabolism of drugs. Certain substances including medications may stimulate this system, while others inhibit it. When this system is *stimulated, it speeds up* metabolism of sensitive medications resulting in lower blood levels and affecting efficacy of the drug. If the system is *inhibited*, metabolism of sensitive drugs is *decreased*, resulting in higher blood levels and possibly increased side effects. For example, drugs that *inhibit the P-450 system,* and therefore decrease metabolism of sensitive drugs, include: erythromycin, cimetidine, propanolol, oral contraceptives, and fluoroquinolones. Drugs that speed up metabolism through *stimulation of the P-450 system* include: phenobarbital, carbamazepine, rifampin, and isoproterenol.

ELIMINATION

The balance between the distribution and the elimination of a drug is termed pharmacokinetics. It is beyond the scope of this course to present a discussion of the mathematical derivations of pharmacokinetics. In general, though, most drugs are metabolized in the liver and excreted through the kidney. Once absorbed into the circulation, drugs reach the liver through the portal circulation and begin the process of elimination before being completely distributed to the site of action. This process is termed *first pass elimination;* it may be counteracted by increasing the dose of the medication administered.

Before excretion, the drug must be transformed to an inactive form that is unable to cross cell membranes. This transformation takes place through two types of reactions. *Phase one reactions* consist of oxidation—the removal of an electron; reduction—the addition of an electron; and hydrolysis—the addition of a water molecule. *Phase two reactions* involve combining the drug with substances that will inactivate it, such as glucuronide, glycine, or sulfate. Immature liver enzymes in the very young child may delay inactivation and elimination of drugs.

Once inactivated, these drugs are then eliminated through the kidneys. Factors that affect excretion in the very young child are immaturity of renal function, glomerulo-tubular imbalance, increased renal vascular resistance, and decreased glomerular filtration (Burns, Brady, Dunn & Starr, 2000; Wynne, Woo & Millard, 2002).

MONITORING DRUG LEVELS

Serum blood samples for the assessment of drug levels measure only the amount of drug absorbed into the circulation, not the amount of drug that reaches a local site of action or the level of active metabolites produced during breakdown of the drug. An example of an active metabolite is caffeine, a breakdown product of theophylline. Blood levels are obtained on drugs which have a narrow *therapeutic range;* that is, a small blood concentration range where the drug is both safe and effective. A drug level that falls below the therapeutic range is ineffective, while a drug level higher than the upper safe limit may be toxic.

Drug levels vary depending on the volume of distribution, elimination, degree of protein binding, and body composition of the patient. Some drug levels (e.g., theophylline) may be drawn in the middle of the dosing schedule, once the drug has reached its steady state; other drugs such as gentamicin may require peak and trough levels to be drawn. In general, trough levels are drawn *half an hour prior* to the dose, and the peak level is drawn *one half to one hour after* an intravenous dose and *one to two hours after* an enterally administered dose. If a trough level is not within the recommended range, the dosing *interval* should be adjusted; if the peak level is not within the recommended range, the *dose* of the medication should be adjusted.

EXAM QUESTIONS

CHAPTER 1
Questions 1–11

1. The most appropriate method of administration of a medication with a short half-life is

   a. single dose.
   b. loading dose followed by a scheduled dosing interval.
   c. intravenous infusion.
   d. oral administration.

2. Absorption is defined as

   a. dissemination of a drug throughout the body.
   b. dissemination of a drug from the circulation to the desired site of action.
   c. movement of the drug into the hepatic circulation.
   d. movement of the drug into the circulation.

3. Instantaneous absorption is provided by

   a. intraventricular administration.
   b. intramuscular injection.
   c. oral liquids.
   d. intravenous infusion.

4. Factors that affect absorption of a medication administered intramuscularly include

   a. muscle perfusion and circulation.
   b. fat tissue and plasma proteins.
   c. body water and fat tissue.
   d. muscle mass and body water.

5. Absorption of an orally administered drug would be affected by

   a. muscle perfusion.
   b. circulation.
   c. GI perfusion.
   d. plasma proteins.

6. A characteristic of the skin of a very young child that affects absorption of topically administered medications is

   a. decreased secretion of sweat.
   b. increased fluid content.
   c. decreased permeability.
   d. decreased skin pH.

7. One factor that affects the dosage of a drug is

   a. bioavailability.
   b. pinocytosis.
   c. protein binding.
   d. the blood-brain barrier.

8. First pass elimination involves

   a. cell membranes.
   b. kidneys.
   c. the integument.
   d. the liver.

7

9. In order to be excreted, a drug must first be

   a. bound to protein.
   b. passed through the liver.
   c. inactivated.
   d. passed through the kidneys.

10. The expected response from stimulation of a b2 receptor site is

    a. vasoconstriction.
    b. vasodilation.
    c. increased peripheral vascular resistance.
    d. elevated heart rate.

11. The term used to describe the effective, safe, circulating level of a drug is

    a. peak level.
    b. therapeutic level.
    c. trough level.
    d. toxic level.

CHAPTER 2

CARDIO-RESPIRATORY DRUGS

CHAPTER OBJECTIVE

After completing this chapter, the reader will be able to specify the classifications of cardio-respiratory medications and indicate the applicable nursing implications for the administration of these drugs.

LEARNING OBJECTIVES

At the completion of the chapter, the reader will be able to

1. recognize which cardiac and respiratory medications are commonly used in the pediatric population.
2. specify common cardio-respiratory conditions in the pediatric population that may benefit from the administration of these medications.
3. recognize common side effects of the use of these medications.

ANTI-ARRHYTHMICS

Factors in pediatric patients that may contribute to arrhythmias include hypoxia, electrolyte and other metabolic imbalances, drug use, and autonomic nervous system problems. In addition to these factors, very young children are at risk for arrhythmias due to immature autonomic innervation, predominance of parasympathetic innervation, and blunted chemical responses that characterize early conduction. These qualities result in a greater incidence of bradycardia and slowed conduction. The conical shape as well as elevated energy demands in the hearts of very young children leaves little reserve available to respond to alterations in pressure or flow. Maturation of the conduction system continues for several months after birth.

Arrhythmias may arise from above the bundle of His; these are called supraventricular arrhythmias. They include supraventricular tachycardia (SVT), Wolf-Parkinson-White (WPW), premature atrial contractions (PACs), atrial fibrillation, and atrial flutter. Wolf-Parkinson-White is a re-entrant phenomenon in which bands of conduction tissue, present prenatally, fail to regress and form abnormal pathways for conduction of the impulse arising in the right atrium. Arrhythmias arising from below the bundle of His are called ventricular arrhythmias and include ventricular tachycardia, ventricular fibrillation, and premature ventricular contractions (PVCs).

Chemically, a conduction impulse in the myocardium is conducted in four phases; anti-arrhythmics are classified according to their function within this chemical structure.

a. *Phase one—the sodium channel phase*—rapid opening of sodium channels allows sodium to move from the extra- to intracellular space.

b. *Phase two—the repolarization phase*—sodium channels close.
c. *Phase three—calcium channel phase*—calcium channels open, allowing calcium and potassium to equilibrate on both sides of the cell membrane.
d. *Phase four—the depolarization phase*—calcium channels close and potassium channels open, allowing potassium to move from the intra- to extracellular space (Harvey & Champe, 1997).

Class 1 - Sodium Channel Blockers

Action: Bind to sodium channel receptor sites to prolong the refractory period and slow heart rate.

Indications: Supraventricular and ventricular arrhythmias and life threatening ventricular arrhythmias; also used after cardioversion to maintain a normal sinus rhythm.

Drugs in class: Quinidine (Duraquin®) class 1-a
flecainide (Tambocor®) class 1-b
lidocaine (Xylocaine®) class 1-c

Lidocaine (Xylocaine)

Pregnancy risk category: B

Contraindications: Heart block, sensitivity to lidocaine or its components.

Side Effects

Cardiovascular: Bradycardia, hypotension, **arrhythmia, cardiovascular collapse.**

Respiratory: Respiratory depression and **respiratory arrest.**

GI-GU: Nausea, vomiting.

Dermatological: None significant.

Hematological: Local thrombophlebitis.

Neurological: Lethargy, coma, agitation, anxiety, **seizures**, confusion, tremor.

Miscellaneous: Tinnitus, blurred vision, **anaphylaxis.**

Food interactions: None significant.

Drug interactions: Cimetidine or beta blockers increase the concentration of lidocaine in the blood, as well as its toxicity (see P-450 enzyme system in Chapter 1); phenytoin and phenobarbital increase cardiac side effects.

Class 2 - Beta Blockers

Action: Block either or both b1 and b2 receptor sites, producing a negative inotropic and chronotropic effect, also increasing blood flow to damaged areas of the myocardium.

Indications: Atrial fibrillation, supraventricular tachycardia, and hypertension.

Drugs in class: Atenolol - b1 (Tenormin®)
metoprolol - b1 (Lopressor®)
esmolol - b1 (Breviblock®)
propranolol - nonspecific, b1 and b2 (Inderal®)
labetalol - a1, b1, b2 (Normodyne®)

Atenolol (Tenormin)

Pregnancy risk category: D

Contraindications: Pulmonary edema, shock, bradycardia, heart block.

Side Effects

Cardiovascular: Bradycardia, hypotension, **heart failure.**

Respiratory: Wheezing, dyspnea, **bronchospasm.**

GI-GU: Constipation, diarrhea, nausea.

Dermatological: Rash.

Hematological: Elevated platelet count.

Neurological: Dizziness, fatigue, lethargy, headache.

Miscellaneous: Fever, leg pain.

Food interactions: none.

Drug interactions: Additive effects if given with antihypertensives; may reverse the effects of theophylline (see P-450 enzyme system in Chapter 1); calcium channel blockers increase cardiac side effects.

Class 3 - Potassium Channel Blockers

Action: Block potassium channels from opening and prevent calcium channels from closing.

Indications: Ventricular arrhythmias.

Drugs in class: Bretylium (Bretylol®).

Bretylium (Bretylol)

Pregnancy risk category: C

Contraindications: Digoxin toxicity, arrhythmias.

Side Effects

>*Cardiovascular:* **Hypotension, bradycardia,** PVCs.
>
>*Respiratory:* Nasal congestion.
>
>*GI-GU:* nausea, Vomiting.
>
>*Dermatological:* Rash.
>
>*Hematological:* None significant.
>
>*Neurological:* Vertigo, confusion, anxiety, syncope.
>
>*Miscellaneous:* Conjunctivitis, hiccups.

Food interactions: None significant.

Drug interactions: Additive effects with other antiarrhythmics.

Class 4 - Calcium Channel Blockers

Action: Block calcium channels, decrease AV node conduction.

Indications: SVTs and hypertension.

Drugs in class: Diltiazem (Cardizem®)—vasodilatory and cardiac effects.
nifedepine (Procardia®)—predominantly vasodilatory effects.
verapamil (Isoptin®)—predominantly cardiac effects.

Nifedepine (Procardia)

Pregnancy risk category: C

Contraindications: Hypersensitivity to the drug or its components.

Side Effects

>*Cardiovascular:* Flushing, hypotension, tachycardia, palpitations, **heart failure.**
>
>*Respiratory:* Shortness of breath, cough.
>
>*GI-GU:* Nausea, vomiting, constipation, gingival hyperplasia.
>
>*Dermatological:* Dermatitis, urticaria.
>
>*Hematological:* **Thrombocytopenia, leukopenia,** anemia, elevated liver enzymes.
>
>*Neurological:* Dizziness, fever, head ache.
>
>*Miscellaneous:* Blurred vision, fever, muscle cramps.

Food interactions: Fat intake may decrease flushing; citrus fruit juice may increase blood levels and toxicity.

Drug interactions: Beta blockers may increase cardiac side effects; cimetidine may increase blood levels; nifedepine increases digoxin levels.

Miscellaneous Anti-Arrhythmics

Digoxin (Lanoxin®)

Pregnancy risk category: C

Action: Promotes movement of calcium from the extracellular to the intracellular space and enhances the action of the vagal nerve; effects are slowed SA and AV conduction and strengthened myocardial contractions.

Indications: Heart failure, supraventricular tachycardia.

Contraindications: Hypersensitivity to the drug or its components, ventricular fibrillation, pericarditis, used with caution in patients with hypoxia, hypothyroidism, and electrolyte imbalance.

Side Effects

>*Cardiovascular:* **Arrhythmia**, SA or AV block.

Respiratory: None significant.

GI-GU: Nausea, abdominal pain, anorexia.

Dermatological: None significant.

Hematological: None significant.

Neurological: Fatigue, weakness, agitation, neuralgia.

Miscellaneous: Photophobia

Food interactions: Fiber and pectin ingestion decreases absorption; avoid licorice as it may increase sodium and water reabsorption and decrease potassium levels.

Drug interactions: Anticholinergics; calcium channel blockers increase serum levels; steroids and diuretics decrease potassium levels resulting in greater risk of digoxin toxicity.

ANTI-HYPERTENSIVES

In the pediatric patient, hypertension is diagnosed if the systolic or diastolic blood pressures are greater than the 95th percentile for age and gender, after three measurements have been taken on separate occasions, in the same arm, with the same equipment, and in the same position. The goals of antihypertensive therapy are to prevent morbidity and mortality and maintain normal blood pressures for age. The major action of antihypertensives is to *decrease preload,* which is defined as the volume of blood presented to the heart prior to systole. Preload is primarily a function of blood volume. *Afterload*, the amount of resistance against which the heart pumps during systole, is a function primarily of peripheral vascular resistance.

The management of hypertension is complicated; several classifications of drugs may be used alone or in combination. Prior to the initiation of medications however, nonpharmacologic therapy such as diet, exercise, and stress reduction are attempted. Diuretics, beta blockers, ACE inhibitors, and vasodilators are among the drugs used in the management of hypertension. Diuretics are discussed in the renal section, and beta blockers are discussed in the cardiac section (Burns, Brady, Dunn & Starr, 2000).

Centrally Acting Nervous System Agents

Action: Stimulate a2 receptor sites to decrease norepinephrine release, decrease conduction, and produce vasodilation.

Drugs in class: Clonidine (Catapres®) - is also used in withdrawal from opiate and nicotine dependence, in the treatment of attention deficit hyperactivity disorder (ADHD), and in the treatment of growth hormone deficiency.

Clonidine (Catapres)

Pregnancy risk category: C

Contraindications: Hypersensitivity to the drug or components.

Side Effects

Cardiovascular: Reynaud's syndrome, hypotension, tachycardia or bradycardia, palpitations, CHF, **severe rebound hypertension** if discontinued abruptly, orthostatic hypotension.

Respiratory: **Respiratory depression** if given through the epidural route.

GI-GU: Constipation, anorexia, dry mouth, nausea, vomiting, urinary retention, impotence.

Dermatological: Rash, pruritus.

Hematological: None significant.

Neurological: Drowsiness, sedation, headache, dizziness, insomnia, anxiety.

Miscellaneous: Sodium and water retention, parotid pain, weight gain.

Food interactions: Minimize sodium and caloric intake; the use of alcohol may increase sedative effects.

Drug interactions: CNS depressants increase sedative effects; beta blockers increase bradycardia or cause paradoxical hypertension.

Peripheral-Acting CNS Agents

Action: Block a1 receptor sites peripherally to produce peripheral vasodilation.

Drugs in class: Prazosin (Minipress®)
terazosin (Hytrin®)

Prazosin (Minipress)

Pregnancy risk category: C

Contraindications: Hypersensitivity to the drug or its components.

Side Effects

    Cardiovascular: Tachycardia, orthostatic hypotension.

    Respiratory: Nasal congestion.

    GI-GU: Nausea, fluid retention, sexual dysfunction.

    Dermatological: Rash.

    Hematological: None significant.

    Neurological: Syncope, dizziness, headache.

    Miscellaneous: Myalgia, fever.

Food interactions: Avoid licorice as it increases sodium and water retention.

Drug interactions: Diuretics and antihypertensives increase CNS effects; NSAIDs decrease antihypertensive effects.

Angiotensin Converting Enzyme (ACE) Inhibitors

Action: Compete for binding sites and prevent conversion of angiotensin 1 to angiotensin 2, a potent vasoconstrictor.

Drugs in class: Enalapril (Vasotec®)
lisinopril (Zestril®)
captopril (Capoten®)—this drug is also used to treat the hypertension that accompanies umbilical arterial catheter-induced clots in newborns. These clots stimulate the renin-angiotensin-aldosterone axis, producing the elevated blood pressure.

Lisinopril (Zestril)

Pregnancy risk category: C first trimester, D second and third trimesters.

Contraindications: Hypersensitivity to the drug or its components.

Side Effects

    Cardiovascular: Hypotension, chest pain

    Respiratory: Dyspnea, cough due to stimulation of bradykin.

    GI-GU: Nausea, diarrhea, decreased taste, vomiting.

    Dermatological: Rash.

    Hematological: **Agranulocytosis, neutropenia.**

    Neurological: Fatigue, dizziness, vertigo, headache.

    Miscellaneous: Muscle cramps, weakness, hyperkalemia.

Food interactions: Limit salt intake, avoid licorice.

Drug interactions: May cause hyperkalemia if taken with potassium-sparing diuretics; NSAIDs and indomethacin may decrease response.

REACTIVE AIRWAY DISEASE

In the pediatric patient, chronic lung and reactive airway disease are among the most common diagnoses. This section will discuss these entities as well as allergic rhinitis.

The underlying pathophysiology of chronic lung disease and reactive airway disease is *inflammation*. Inflammation leads to endothelial damage, fibrosis, and edema. In the older child, reactive airway disease is the result of a cascade of events, beginning with exposure to triggers such as dust mites, pollens, and animal dander. These triggers initiate the release of substances that mediate the inflammatory response. These mediators include:

a. Mast cells—bind to IgE, an immunoglobulin, rupturing the mast cell and releasing histamine, a bronchoconstrictor.

b. White cells—macrophages, lymphocytes, neutrophils, and eosinophils are released in response to a trigger, causing inflammation of the airways.

c. Leukotrienes—cause airway edema and bronchoconstriction.

The goals of therapy in these children are to decrease inflammation and edema with short-acting drugs, maintain normal lung function and activity level, and prevent exacerbations with longer acting drugs. Many of these drugs are administered by metered dose inhaler, with or without a spacer (Steinbach, 2000; Turcios, 2001).

A metered dose inhaler (MDI) provides smaller drug particles for dissemination into smaller airways. The use of the MDI must be coordinated with inhalation and therefore is recommended for children over five years of age; for younger children a spacer is added. The use of a nebulizer with a mask is recommended for children less than one year. It is important to teach the child and parent the correct use of the equipment.

Using an MDI

- Shake the inhaler;
- take a deep breath and let it out;
- place the inhaler 1–2 inches from the mouth, release the dose, and inhale (if using inhaled corticosteroids [ICS], or dry powder, the inhaler should be placed in the mouth);
- if more than one puff has been ordered, wait about one minute between puffs;
- if using ICS, rinse the mouth after use to prevent oral thrush; and
- if using short-acting beta agonists with an inhaled steroid, use the short-acting beta agonists first to open airways before using the inhaled steroid.

Adding a Spacer

- Shake the inhaler;
- connect the MDI to the end of the spacer and remove the mouth piece covering from the spacer;
- take a deep breath and let it out;
- place the end of the spacer into the mouth, release the dose, and inhale to a count of five;
- if more than one puff has been ordered, wait about one minute between puffs; and
- if using ICS, rinse the mouth after use to prevent oral thrush.

Short-Acting Beta 2 Agonists

Action: Stimulate beta 2 receptors to produce vaso- and bronchodilation, relax smooth muscles, and inhibit mast cell rupture.

Indications: Acute episodes of asthma, bronchospasm, exercise-induced asthma.

Drugs in class: albuterol (Proventil®, Ventolin®)
terbutaline (Brethaire®)
isoetharine (Bronkosol®)—a nonspecific beta agonist, stimulates b1 and b2 sites.
levalbuterol (Xopenex™)—a newer drug, longer acting than albuterol, but with fewer side effects.
ipratropium (Combivent®, albuterol)—a new drug that combines the effects of a short-acting beta 2 agonist with an anticholinergic.

Albuterol (Proventil, Ventolin)

Pregnancy risk category: C

Contraindications: Hypersensitivity to the drug or its components, use with caution in patients

Chapter 2–
Cardio-Respiratory Drugs

with diabetes mellitus, hypertension, hyperthyroidism, seizures, or cardiac abnormalities.

Side Effects

Cardiovascular: Tachycardia, hypertension, palpitations, chest pain.

Respiratory: Cough, irritated oropharynx, **bronchospasm**.

GI-GU: GI upset, nausea, vomiting, altered taste.

Dermatological: Urticaria.

Hematological: Hypokalemia.

Neurological: CNS stimulation, tremors, weakness, hyperactivity, and insomnia, especially in younger children.

Miscellaneous: Muscle cramping, diaphoresis.

Food interactions: None significant.

Drug interactions: Effects are antagonized by beta blockers, MAO inhibitors, and tricyclic antidepressants increase effects.

Long-Acting Beta 2 Agonists

Action: Similar to shorter acting beta agonists, but slower onset of action and longer duration.

Indications: Prevention of exacerbations of asthma, maintenance therapy of acute asthma and COPD, prevention of exercise-induced bronchospasm.

* These drugs are not indicated for acute episodes.

Drugs in class: salmeterol (Serevent®)
fluticasone and salmeterol (Advair®, Diskus®)—a newer combination drug
formeterol (Foradil®)—will replace salmeterol. This new drug replaces the CFC (chlorofluorocarbon) propellant in salmeterol with the newer HFA (hydrofluoroalkane) to reduce environmental damage

Salmeterol (Serevent)

Pregnancy risk category: C

Contraindications: Sensitivity to the drug or its components,* *not indicated for acute episodes.*

Side Effects

Cardiovascular: Prolonged QT interval, tachycardia, **ventricular arrhythmias,** palpitations.

Respiratory: Cough, pharyngitis, **respiratory arrest, bronchospasm.**

GI-GU: GI upset, diarrhea, nausea.

Dermatological: Rash, pruritis.

Hematological: None.

Neurological: Dizziness, headache, hyperactivity, insomnia.

Miscellaneous: Joint pain.

Food interactions: None significant.

Drug interactions: Additive effects with beta adrenergics; effects decreased with beta blockers; MAO inhibitors and tricyclic antidepressants increase cardiac side effects.

Inhaled Corticosteroids

Action: Decrease inflammation by inhibiting mediators; decrease edema and mucous production.

Indications: In asthma for long-term prevention, also given in oral or IV form for acute exacerbations that are nonresponsive to short-acting beta agonists. When taking inhaled steroids, it is important to teach patients and families to rinse the inhaler weekly, rinse the patient's mouth after each dose to prevent oral thrush, and warm the canister before use. Growth parameters should also be checked routinely while the child is on steroid therapy, although this risk is greater with systemic steroids compared to inhaled steroids.

*These drugs are not indicated for acute episodes.

Drugs in class: beclomethasone (Vanceril®)
flunisolide (Aerobid®)

triamcinolone (Azmacort®)

fluticasone (Flovent®)—also used topically for acne

prednisone and methylprednisolone are given orally or IV

*budesonide (Pulmicort®)—as of August 2000, this drug is now the corticosteroid of choice, and now comes in a form called respules, which has been approved for children from 1–8 years of age.

Budesonide (Pulmicort, Pulmicort Respules)

Pregnancy risk category: C

Contraindications: Sensitivity to the drug or components, **not indicated for acute episodes.**

Side Effects

Cardiovascular: Facial edema.

Respiratory: Cough, epistaxis, rhinitis, sinusitis, **bronchospasm**.

GI-GU: Dry mouth, altered taste, GI upset, nausea, growth suppression.

Dermatological: Rash, pruritus, oral candidiasis.

Hematological: None significant.

Neurological: Nervousness, migraine, insomnia, headache.

Miscellaneous: Side effects are dose and route dependent as a result of hypothalamic-pituitary-axis suppression.

Food interactions: None significant.

Drug interactions: Ketoconazole may increase serum levels.

* note on inhaled corticosteroids (ICS)—some ICSs have a longer duration of action and the risk of "stacking" doses is a real one when frequent doses are taken. Patient teaching should include the duration of action and the recommended number of doses for each specific drug.

Mast Cell Stabilizers

Action: Stabilize mast cells, prevent release of histamine.

Indications: Allergic rhinitis; requires two to three weeks for effect, so not used in acute episodes; prophylactic long-term therapy of asthma; prevention of exercise-induced asthma.

Drugs in class: cromolyn (Nasalcrom®, Intal®)
nedocromil (Tilade®)

Cromolyn (Nasalcrom, Intal)

Pregnancy risk category: B

Contraindications: Sensitivity to the drug or components.

Side Effects

Cardiovascular: None.

Respiratory: Cough, wheeze, sneezing, nasal congestion, irritated oropharyngitis.

GI-GU: Unpleasant taste, nausea, vomiting, diarrhea, dry mouth.

Dermatological: Rash, angioedema, urticaria.

Hematological: None.

Neurological: Dizziness, headache.

Miscellaneous: Nasal burning, ocular stinging or lacrimation with ophthalmic preparations, arthralgia.

Food interactions: None significant.

Drug interactions: None significant.

Anticholinergics

Action: Blocks acetylcholine at parasympathetic sites to produce bronchodilation, decreased vagal tone, and decreased mucous secretion.

Indications: Asthma and bronchospasm seen in bronchitis and COPD, allergic rhinitis.

Drugs in class: Ipratropium (Atrovent)

Ipratropium (Atrovent)

Pregnancy risk category: B

Contraindications: Sensitivity to the drug, atropine, or soy and peanut products, not indicated for acute episodes.

Side Effects

* poorly absorbed from the lungs so side effects are rare

Cardiovascular: Palpitations, tachycardia, flushing, hypertension or hypotension.

Respiratory: Cough, hoarseness, epistaxis, dry secretions.

GI-GU: Nausea, constipation, dysuria.

Dermatological: Rash, pruritus, alopecia.

Hematological: None significant.

Neurological: Nervousness, dizziness, headache, fatigue, insomnia.

Miscellaneous: Blurred vision, back pain.

Food interactions: None significant.

Drug interactions: Additive effects with other anticholinergics.

Leukotriene Modifiers

Action: Inhibit the release of leukotrienes to decrease bronchoconstriction and airway edema.

Drugs in class: zafirlukast (Accolate®)
 zileuton (Zyflo®)
 monteleukast (Singulair®)

Montelukast (Singulair)

Pregnancy risk category: B

Contraindications: Hypersensitivity to the drug or its components.

Side Effects

Cardiovascular: None significant.

Respiratory: Nasal congestion, sinusitis, cough, laryngitis.

GI-GU: Diarrhea, nausea, abdominal pain.

Dermatological: Rash.

Hematological: Elevated liver enzymes.

Neurological: Headache, fever, dizziness.

Miscellaneous: Otitis, increased susceptibility to viral infections.

Food interactions: Tablet form contains phenylalanine.

Drug interactions: NSAIDs may increase GI upset; phenobarbital and rifampin decrease blood levels.

ALLERGIES

Often reactive airway disease co-exists with allergies or is exacerbated by an allergic response to triggers. Allergic reactions are mediated by an IgE response, which ruptures mast cells, causing histamine release and increased secretions. Allergies and the allergic rhinitis that may accompany them are seasonal and treated with mast cell stabilizers, anticholinergics, and inhaled steroids, discussed previously, as well as with antihistamines and decongestants.

Decongestants and antihistamines may interact with prescription drugs or exacerbate underlying medical conditions such as diabetes, hypertension, and cardiac disease, so they should be used with caution in these states. Drugs of choice in the treatment of allergies when these conditions co-exist include mast cell stabilizers and short-term use of antihistamines (Burns, Brady, Dunn & Starr, 2000).

Decongestants

Action: a1 agonists that cause vaso- and pulmonary constriction and decreased nasal congestion.

Indications: Nasal congestion, allergic rhinitis.

Drugs in class: Pseudoephedrine (Sudafed®)
 Oxymetazoline (Afrin®)

Oxymetazoline (Afrin)

Pregnancy risk category: C

Contraindications: Sensitivity to the drug, MAO inhibitor therapy, caution in use with patients with cardiac conditions, hypertension, or diabetes mellitus.

Side Effects

> *Cardiovascular:* Hypertension, palpitations, pallor, reflex bradycardia.
>
> *Respiratory:* Sneezing, rebound congestion (medicamentosa rhinitis) if used for longer than three days, dry mucous membranes.
>
> *GI-GU:* Nausea, vomiting.
>
> *Dermatological:* None significant.
>
> *Hematological:* None significant.
>
> *Neurological:* Nervousness, dizziness, headache, CNS depression, tremor.
>
> *Miscellaneous:* Ocular stinging, blurred vision, diaphoresis.

Food interactions: None.

Drug interactions: Use of anesthesia while on these drugs may result in myocardial sensitivity; methyldopa, MAO inhibitors, and tricyclic antidepressants increase hypertensive effects.

Antihistamines

Action: Inhibition of histamine 1 receptor sites.

Indications: Congestion and itching in allergic rhinitis, or chronic urticaria; sedative effects are useful for insomnia.

Drugs in class: fexofenadine (Allegra®)
loratadine (Claritin®)
diphenhydramine (Benadryl®)
cetirizine (Zyrtec™)

Cetirizine (Zyrtec)

Pregnancy risk category: B

Contraindications: Sensitivity to the drug or its components, caution in patients with renal or liver problems.

Side Effects

Cardiovascular: None significant.

Respiratory: Cough, epistaxis, **bronchospasm.**

GI-GU: Diarrhea or constipation, abdominal pain, dry mouth, pharyngitis.

Dermatological: None significant.

Hematological: None significant.

Neurological: Headache, drowsiness, depression, confusion, paresthesia, hypertonia, leg cramps, tremor.

Miscellaneous: May cause paradoxical excitement in children.

Food interactions: None significant.

Drug interactions: Anticholinergics increase side effects.

Antitussives

Indications: Cough

Action: Irritates GI mucosa and stimulates respiratory tract, increasing respiratory fluid volume and thinning secretions.

Drugs in class: Guaifenesin

Guaifenesin

Pregnancy risk category: C

Contraindications: Sensitivity to the drug.

Side Effects

> *Cardiovascular:* None significant.
>
> *Respiratory:* None significant.
>
> *GI-GU:* Nausea and vomiting.
>
> *Dermatological:* Rash.
>
> *Hematological:* None significant.
>
> *Neurological:* Drowsiness, headache.
>
> *Miscellaneous:* None significant.

Food interactions: None significant.

Drug interactions: Some preparations contain dextromethorphan, which may cause hypotension in patients receiving anti-hypertensive medication.

Methylxanthines

Indications: Used in asthma as a bronchodilator, also in apnea of prematurity.

Actions: Stimulate respiratory center, decrease carbon dioxide threshold by inhibition of adenosine and release of calcium.

Drugs in class: theophylline

> Aminophylline—given IV or IM, can also be given PO.
> caffeine—has less effect on lower esophageal sphincter tone; given as the citrate formulation as the benzoate form competes for bilirubin binding sites, leading to hyperbilirubinemia.

Precaution with methylxanthines: Serum levels must be measured with these drugs as they have a narrow therapeutic range; if signs of toxicity are noted, including vomiting, levels should be drawn and the next dose held until levels are available. **Because aminophylline and theophylline are not equivalent in action, when changing from intravenous aminophylline to oral theophylline, the oral theophylline dose should be increased by twenty per cent over the intravenous dose.** This is due to the decreased bioavailability of the oral formulation.

Theophylline

Pregnancy risk category: C

Contraindications: Sensitivity to the drug or its components.

Side Effects

> *Side effects are dose dependent.*
>
> *Cardiovascular:* Tachycardia, occasional PVCs at high doses, **arrhythmia**, palpitations.
>
> *Respiratory:* Tachypnea, **respiratory arrest.**
>
> *GI-GU:* GI upset, reflux, diarrhea, vomiting, abdominal pain, nausea.
>
> *Dermatological:* None.
>
> *Hematological:* Elevated free fatty acids.
>
> *Neurological:* Nervousness, headache, insomnia, agitation, dizziness, **seizures at high doses.**
>
> *Miscellaneous:* Tremor, muscle cramp, may cause learning disabilities in children.

Food interactions: Food does not affect the absorption of theophylline or aminophylline, however, may cause a "dose dumping" of sustained release formulation.

Drug interactions: Theophylline and aminophylline have significant interactions with food and drugs. Caffeine is a metabolite of theophylline and has fewer interactions.

The following is a *partial list* of the most important food and drug interactions related to theophylline and aminophylline.

The following conditions may *increase* serum theophylline/aminophylline levels:

- Pulmonary edema.
- Congestive heart failure.
- Fever.
- Hypothyroidism.
- Renal failure in children under three months of age.
- Viral illness.

The following conditions may *decrease* serum theophylline/aminophylline levels:

- Smoking.
- Excessive intake of carbohydrates or protein.
- Intake of charcoal broiled foods.

The following drugs may *increase* theophylline/aminophylline levels:

- Alcohol.
- Beta blockers.
- Cimetidine.
- Corticosteroids.
- Macrolide antibiotics.
- Loop diuretics.

- Oral contraceptives.
- Thyroid hormones.

The following drugs may *decrease* theophylline/aminophylline levels:

- Phenobarbital.
- Phenytoin.
- Rifampin.
- Loop diuretics.
- Carbamazepine.

Theophylline/aminophylline may have the following effects on drugs:

- *Decrease serum levels of*
    — benzodiazepines;
    — adenosine;
    — esmolol;
    — zafirlukast; and
    — lithium.
- *Increase side effects of*
    ephedrine; and
    halothane.

EXAM QUESTIONS

CHAPTER 2
Questions 12–20

12. The classification of drug used in arrhythmias but *contraindicated* in asthma is

    a. sodium channel blockers.
    b. non-specific beta blockers.
    c. potassium channel blockers.
    d. calcium channel blockers.

13. One of the main goals of treatment of hypertension in the pediatric patient is

    a. increase preload.
    b. increase afterload.
    c. decrease preload.
    d. decrease afterload.

14. The underlying pathophysiology of reactive airway disease that is considered in administration of medications is

    a. insufficient surfactant.
    b. increased parasympathetic innervation.
    c. inflammation.
    d. increased peripheral vascular resistance.

15. Side effects of prednisone treatment are a result of

    a. nonspecific beta receptor site stimulation.
    b. hypothalamic-pituitary-adrenal axis suppression.
    c. rebound congestion.
    d. inhibition of histamine release.

16. Two classes of drug that are *contraindicated* during *acute* asthma are

    a. short-acting beta two agonists and PO corticosteroids.
    b. beta blockers and aminophylline.
    c. mast cell stabilizers and long-acting beta 2 blockers.
    d. short-acting beta two agonists and anticholinergics.

17. A side effect of the use of decongestants such as oxymetazoline (Afrin) is

    a. liver impairment.
    b. ventricular arrhythmias.
    c. growth delay.
    d. medicamentosa rhinitis.

18. The dose change required when changing from an intravenous aminophylline dose of 10 mg to oral theophylline is

    a. 12 mg.
    b. 1.2 mg.
    c. 10 mg.
    d. 10.2 mg.

19. In teaching patients and families about the use of an inhaled steroid by MDI, it is important to stress

    a. the inhaler should be used immediately during acute episodes.
    b. they should rinse their mouth after each dose.
    c. inhaled steroids should never be mixed with other medications.
    d. if using short-acting beta agonists with an inhaled steroid, use the steroid first.

20. One physiological situation that *decreases* serum theophylline/aminophylline levels is

    a. fever.
    b. smoking.
    c. viral illness.
    d. hypothyroidism.

CHAPTER 3

GENITOURINARY, GASTROINTESTINAL AND ENDOCRINE MEDICATIONS

CHAPTER OBJECTIVE

After completing this chapter, the reader will be able to specify the classifications of gastrointestinal and genitourinary medications and indicate the applicable nursing implications for the administration of these drugs.

LEARNING OBJECTIVES

At the completion of the chapter, the reader will be able to

1. recognize which gastrointestinal and genitourinary medications are commonly used in the pediatric population.
2. recognize common side effects of the use of these medications.

DIURETICS

The functions of the kidney are filtration, water, electrolyte and acid-base balance, and blood pressure regulation. Aldosterone, antidiuretic hormone, and electrolyte gradients are the major regulators of fluid and electrolyte balance. A feedback mechanism exists to maintain equilibrium between these three systems. As the filtrate flows from the glomerulus to the proximal tubules, amino acids, bicarbonate, sodium, and glucose are filtered out. In the loop of Henle, water and sodium are either retained or excreted as needed. As the filtrate moves through the distal and collecting tubules, sodium is exchanged for potassium and hydrogen ions through the action of aldosterone, and water is either excreted or reabsorbed as needed under the influence of antidiuretic hormone. Diuretics are given in conditions of fluid overload, such as renal failure, certain cardiac conditions, and chronic lung disease.

Thiazide Diuretics

Action: Inhibit sodium and chloride reabsorption in the distal tubules, resulting in enhanced excretion of sodium and water.

Indications: Edema, hypertension, cardiac disease.

Drugs in class: Chlorothiazide (Diuril®), hydrochlorothiazide (Hydrodiuril®).

Hydrochlorothiazide (Hydrodiuril)

Pregnancy risk category: B

Contraindications: Sensitivity to the drug or its components, anuria.

Side Effects

   Cardiovascular: Orthostatic hypotension.

   Respiratory: Respiratory distress.

   GI-GU: Nausea, vomiting, cramping, diarrhea, anorexia, **pancreatitis, renal failure,** hepatitis.

   Dermatological: Photosensitivity, alopecia, rash.

   Hematological: **Aplastic and hemolytic ane-**

mias, agranulocytosis, leukopenia, **thrombocytopenia,** jaundice.

Neurological: Weakness, paresthesia, drowsiness, headache, dizziness.

Miscellaneous: Hypokalemia, hyperglycemia, hypochloremic metabolic acidosis, hyperlipidemia, hyperuricemia, **anaphylactic reactions.**

Food interactions: Fiber and pectin intake may decrease absorption.

Drug interactions: Decreases effects of antidiabetic agents; decreases lithium clearance; NSAIDs decrease the antihypertensive effects; cholestyramine decreases absorption.

Loop Diuretics

Action: Inhibit reabsorption of electrolytes in the ascending loop of Henle; these are the strongest diuretics.

Indications: These fast-acting diuretics are used in acute pulmonary edema and facilitate calcium excretion in hypercalcemia.

Drugs in class: Furosemide (Lasix®)
　　　　　　　　ethacrynic acid

Furosemide (Lasix)

Pregnancy risk category: C

Contraindications: Hypersensitivity to the drug or its components; anuria, although may be given to newborns with anuria after a fluid challenge.

Side Effects

Cardiovascular: Orthostatic hypotension.

Respiratory: None significant.

GI-GU: Nausea, anorexia, vomiting, cramping, constipation, nephrocalcinosis, prerenal azotemia, hypercalciuria; oral solutions contain sorbitol and may cause diarrhea, hyperglycemia.

Dermatological: Urticaria, photosensitivity.

Hematological: **Agranulocytosis, anemia, thrombocytopenia,** elevated cholesterol, jaundice.

Neurological: Dizziness, headache.

Miscellaneous: Ototoxicity, hypokalemia, hyponatremia, hypochloremia, alkalosis, dehydration, nephrocalcinosis, blurred vision.

Food interactions: Do not mix with acidic foods; limit intake of licorice (increases sodium and water retention and potassium losses).

Drug interactions: Decreases lithium clearance; decreases glucose tolerance with antidiabetic agents; effects decreased with intake of indomethacin; increased ototoxicity with aminoglycoside antibiotics; may increase effectiveness of warfarin.

Potassium-Sparing Diuretics

Action: Inhibit sodium and potassium exchange in the collecting tubules.

Indications: Hypertension or in conditions in which aldosterone levels are high.

Drugs in class: amiloride (Midamor®)
　　　　　　　　spironolactone (Aldactone®)
　　　　　　　　triamterene (Dyrenium®)

Spironolactone (Aldactone)

Pregnancy risk category: D

Contraindications: Sensitivity to the drug or components, renal failure, anuria, hyperkalemia.

Side Effects

Cardiovascular: **Arrhythmia.**

Respiratory: Cough, shortness of breath, dyspnea.

GI-GU: Nausea, vomiting, diarrhea, cramping, gastric bleeding, dysuria,

Dermatological: Rash, urticaria.

Hematological: **Agranulocytosis,** elevated BUN.

Neurological: Lethargy, headache, mental confusion, weakness, paresthesia.

Miscellaneous: Hyperkalemia, hyponatremia, hyperchloremic metabolic acidosis, amenorrhea, breast tenderness, increased hair growth in females, gynecomastia in males.

Food interactions: Avoid licorice and salt substitutes.

Drug interactions: Potassium and other potassium-sparing diuretics and ACE inhibitors may increase serum potassium levels; decreases digoxin clearance; decreases effects of anticoagulants.

Carbonic Anhydrase Inhibitors

Action: Inhibits carbonic anhydrase in the proximal tubules, a mild diuretic.

Indications: Glaucoma and epilepsy.

Side Effects: Drowsiness, nephrocalcinosis, potassium depletion.

Drugs in class: Acetazolamide (Diamox®).

Acetazolamide (Diamox)

Pregnancy risk category: C

Contraindications: Hypersensitivity to the drug or components; hepatic disease, adrenal insufficiency, or severe renal disease.

Side Effects

Cardiovascular: None significant.

Respiratory: Cyanosis, hyperpnea.

GI-GU: GI irritation, anorexia, nausea, vomiting, melena, dry mouth, metallic taste.

Dermatological: Rash, **erythema multiforme, Stevens-Johnson syndrome,** photosensitivity.

Hematological: **Bone marrow suppression, thrombocytopenia, hemolytic anemia, agranulocytosis, hypokalemia, hyperglycemia,** hyperchloremic metabolic acidosis.

Neurological: Drowsiness, fatigue, dizziness, depression, fever, seizures, muscle weakness, paresthesia.

Miscellaneous: Hepatic insufficiency, renal calculi, phosphaturia, myopia

Food interactions: None significant.

Drug interactions: Decreases excretion of tricyclic antidepressants; increases excretion of lithium, salicylates, and phenobarbital; may increase osteomalacia with salicylates and phenobarbital.

Osmotic Diuretics

Action: Create an osmotic diuresis with minimal salt loss.

Indications: Increased intracranial pressure, used also to increase urine flow in ingestion of toxic substances. These medications are given intravenously.

Drugs in class: Mannitol
urea

Mannitol

Pregnancy risk category: C

Contraindications: Sensitivity to the drug or components, severe renal disease, active intracranial hemorrhage, severe pulmonary edema.

Side Effects

Cardiovascular: **CHF** due to circulatory overload.

Respiratory: Pulmonary edema.

GI-GU: Dry mouth, urinary retention.

Dermatological: None significant.

Hematological: Fluid and electrolyte imbalance and dehydration.

Neurological: **Seizures,** headache, dizziness.

Miscellaneous: Allergic reactions, local tissue necrosis with intravenous infiltration.

Food interactions: Avoid excess water intake.

Drug interactions: Lithium increases excretion.

PRIMARY NOCTURNAL ENURESIS

Diurnal or daytime enuresis is defined as unintentional leakage of urine during the daytime in a child old enough to be bladder trained. The majority of children are toilet trained by about four years, and diurnal enuresis is diagnosed after this age. Causes include structural defects, urinary tract infection, constipation, emotional distress, and diabetes mellitus.

However, the most common type of enuresis in children is *primary nocturnal enuresis* (PNE), which is defined as unintentional leakage of urine at night. Nocturnal enuresis has a familial association, is diagnosed in children over the age of six years, and in only about three percent of children is there an organic cause. PNE is attributed to

- deep sleep or inability to awaken with feelings of bladder fullness;
- small bladder capacity; and
- decreased ADH levels.

Antidiuretic hormone usually undergoes a surge during the night resulting in decreased urine production. In some children, this surge does not occur, leading to greater urine production. Nonpharmacologic methods of treatment are most successful and include bladder stretching exercises, enuresis alarm systems, behavior modification, and limiting intake of liquids before bedtime.

Drugs used to treat PNE include desmopressin (DDAVP), a vasopressor that increases water reabsorption in the distal tubules and concentrates urine; imipramine (Tofranil®) a tricyclic antidepressant (*see* Psychiatric drug section) that increases bladder capacity through its anticholinergic effects, and oxybutynin, an anticholinergic drug that decreases urine production and detrussor muscle contractions. These drugs are usually used short-term only, and relapse rates after discontinuation are greater than 90% (Hogg et al., 2000).

Desmopressin (DDAVP)

Pregnancy risk category: B

Contraindications: Sensitivity to the drug or its components, Von Willebrand's disease or hemophilia.

Side Effects

Cardiovascular: Hypertension, palpitations, tachycardia, chest pain, facial flushing.

Respiratory: Rhinitis, upper respiratory infections, epistaxis, nasal congestion.

GI-GU: Nausea, abdominal cramps, vomiting, vulval pain, balanitis.

Dermatological: None significant.

Hematological: None significant.

Neurological: Headache, dizziness, agitation, insomnia.

Miscellaneous: Hyponatremia, water intoxication, itchy eyes.

Food interactions: None significant.

Drug interactions: Decreased effects with lithium.

GASTROESOPHAGEAL REFLUX

Gastroesophageal reflux disease (GERD) is a condition seen in children as well as adults. The underlying pathophysiology is ineffective lower esophageal sphincter (LES) tone and delayed emptying time. Causes may be related to structural defects such as hiatal hernia or tracheoesophageal fistula, chemical irritation from drugs, smoking, or alcohol consumption. The ineffective LES is not sufficient to counteract elevated intra-abdominal pressure generated during digestion, allowing backward, or retrograde, flow of acidic gastric contents into the esophagus. GERD may lead to esophagitis due to acidity of gastric contents, and it has been implicated in apnea in the very young child. The combination of mechanical obstruction from refluxed material and the chemical irritation results in an apneic event. Symptoms of GERD may include poor weight gain, vomiting, and recurrent pneumonia, particularly in the right upper lobe. Older pediatric patients may complain of midchest pain or heartburn that worsens with meals or when lying down.

The goal of drug therapy is to increase LES and gastric emptying time, as well as decrease acidity. Gastric acid is produced when acetylcholine, gastrin, and histamine receptors are stimulated, activating the proton pump mechanism to secreting gastric acid. Medications utilized to block this mechanism include antacids, H2 antagonists, proton pump inhibitors, and prokinetics (Burns, Brady, Dunn & Starr, 2000).

Antacids

Action: Neutralize acidity of reflux fluid.

Indications: Treatment of mild GERD.

Drugs in class: Aluminum salts (Amphogel®)
magnesium salts (Milk of Magnesia®)—also used in treatment of encopresis, hypertension, and hypomagnesemia, seizures associated with acute nephritis
alginic acid (sucralfate)
simethicone (Gaviscon®)

Magnesium Salts (Milk of Magnesia)

Pregnancy risk category: B

Contraindications: Severe renal impairment, myocardial damage, ileostomy, or colostomy, intestinal obstruction, appendicitis, abdominal pain.

Side effects: *side effects are related to magnesium levels.

>3 mg/dl - depressed CNS, blocked neuromuscular transmission.

>5 mg/dl - depressed deep tendon reflexes, flushing, somnolence.

>12 mg/dl - **respiratory paralysis, complete heart block.**

Cardiovascular: Hypotension.

Respiratory: See above.

GI-GU: Abdominal cramping, gas formation.

Dermatological: Not significant.

Hematological: Hypermagnesemia (see above).

Neurological: See above.

Miscellaneous: Muscle weakness.

Food interactions: Not significant.

Drug interactions: Decreases the absorption of H2 antagonists, phenytoin, iron salts, benzodiazepines, steroids; *enhances* the effects of calcium channel blockers and neuromuscular blockers; *additive effect* with CNS depressants.

H2 Antagonists

Action: Inhibit histamine release from H2 receptors.

Indications: Gastric acidity.

Drugs in class: famotidine (Pepcid®)
ranitidine (Zantac®)
cimetidine (Tagamet®)

Ranitidine (Zantac)

Pregnancy risk category: B

Contraindications: Sensitivity to the drug, components, or other H2 antagonists, acute porphyria.

Side Effects

Cardiovascular: Bradycardia, tachycardia.

Respiratory: Not significant.

GI-GU: Constipation, nausea, vomiting, abdominal discomfort.

Dermatological: Rash, alopecia, erythema multiforme.

Hematological: Thrombocytopenia, **granulocytopenia, leukopenia,** increased creatinine.

Neurological: Dizziness, sedation, mental confusion, headache.

Miscellaneous: Hepatitis, pain at injection site, arthralgias, gynecomastia.

Food interactions: Not significant.

Drug interactions: Absorption decreased with antacids, decreases absorption of diazepam, antifungals; increases effects of warfarin.

Proton Pump Inhibitors

Action: Inhibit hydrogen and potassium ion pump systems to decrease secretion of gastric acid.

Indications: For short-term therapy of GERD.

Side effects: Long-term therapy increases the risk of gastric cancer, can decrease levels of folic acid and B12, and increase bacterial growth.

Drugs in class: lansoprazole (Prevacid®)
omeprazole (Prilosec®)

Omeprazole - Prilosec

Pregnancy risk category: C

Contraindications: Sensitivity to the drug or components.

Side Effects

Cardiovascular: Chest pain, tachycardia, bradycardia, palpitations.

Respiratory: Pharyngeal pain, cough, epistaxis.

GI-GU: Diarrhea, nausea, abdominal pain, vomiting, constipation, flatulence, dry mouth anorexia, urinary frequency.

Dermatological: Rash, dry skin.

Hematological: **Agranulocytosis, thrombocytopenia,** anemia, **leukocytosis**, hypoglycemia.

Neurological: Headache, dizziness, insomnia, anxiety, fever.

Miscellaneous: Hepatitis, jaundice.

Food interactions: Not significant.

Drug interactions: Drug interactions are based in inhibition of oxidative metabolism; decreases absorption of antifungals, iron, and ampicillin; decreases clearance of diazepam, phenytoin, and warfarin; increases absorption of digoxin.

Prokinetics

Action: Increase LES tone, increase gastric emptying time and peristalsis.

Indications: First line treatment for GERD.

Drugs in class: metoclopramide (Reglan®)
cisapride (Propulcid®)—this drug is no longer in use because it prolongs the QT interval, leading to cardiac arrhythmias.

Metoclopramide - Reglan

Pregnancy risk category: B

Contraindications: Sensitivity to the drug or components, history of seizure disorder, or medications with extrapyramidal reactions.

Side Effects

Cardiovascular: Hyper- or hypotension, SVT, bradycardia, **A-V block.**

Respiratory: Not significant.

GI-GU: Constipation, diarrhea, urinary frequency, impotence.

Dermatological: Not significant.

Hematological: Methemoglobinemia, neutropenia, leukopenia, agranulocytosis.

Neurological: Drowsiness, fatigue, anxiety, extrapyramidal reactions (mostly in children at high intravenous doses), hallucinations, dystonia.

Miscellaneous: Porphyria, visual disturbances, hypersensitivity reactions, gynecomastia, amenorrhea, galactorrhea, hyperprolactinemia.

Food interactions: Not significant.

Drug interactions: Decreases digoxin and cimetidine absorption; increases cyclosporin absorption; increases hypertensive reactions with

MAOIs; enhances effects of neuromuscular blocking agents.

NUTRITIONAL SUPPLEMENTS

In the pediatric patient, providing adequate nutrition for growth while minimizing free water intake in conditions such as chronic lung disease and cardiac compromise is often a delicate balance. The major nutrients required for growth include carbohydrates, lipids (fats), and proteins. Carbohydrates should comprise about 40–50% of the daily intake of calories; they are the major nutritional substrate for the brain. Fats should comprise about 30% in children, but about 50% in infants, and are vital for myelinization of nerves (cholesterol) and absorption of fat soluble vitamins (A, D, E, and K). Proteins should comprise about 20–30% of daily caloric intake.

Glucose is digested in the intestines by an enzyme, lactase. Very young children are deficient in lactase but its production may be stimulated with dexamethasone, a steroid, or human growth factor, an endogenous substance. Glucose polymers, such as polycose, are administered enterally to increase caloric density for weight gain while minimizing free water intake in conditions that require fluid restriction.

Digestion of lipids begins in the mouth with the enzyme lipase and continues in the stomach in the presence of gastric lipase, which functions well in the acidic environment of the stomach and does not require the presence of bile salts. Intestinal digestion of lipids may be limited in the young child because of decreased bile salts and intestinal lipase and a delayed secretory response to the presence of lipids at this site. Lipids are supplemented orally in the form of *medium-chain triglycerides,* which are absorbed directly through the gastric mucosa. An intravenous form is also available for children who require parenteral nutritional supplementation.

The digestion of proteins is limited in the young child due to insufficient levels of pepsin and enterokinase. In order to maintain growth and a positive nitrogen balance, about 3 grams per kilogram of body weight per day of protein should be provided. An oral protein supplement, Promod, is available. These supplements are added to either expressed breast milk or formula to supplement calories. The sequence for adding supplements is usually glucose supplements first, followed by fat supplements next, and finally protein supplements. The amount of each supplement depends on the required caloric intake (Young & Magnum, 2002).

DIABETIC MEDICATIONS

Diabetes is defined as a relative or absolute lack of insulin and is diagnosed when a fasting blood sugar is greater than 126 mg/dl on two separate tests. Glucose is absorbed into the blood stream from the intestines and carried across the cellular membrane by insulin. In the absence of insulin, glucose is unable to cross the membrane and builds up in the blood. The osmotic pressure created results in diuresis, thirst, and dehydration. Consequently, fatty acids and protein are broken down to provide nutrition for the cells, resulting in ketosis, ketonuria, and weight loss. The goals of therapy for diabetics are to: Maintain a normal blood glucose level, maintain normal activities, and prevent or minimize the sequelae of the disease such as vascular compromise.

Diabetes classifications are based on etiology:

- Type 1a - autoimmune-mediated, with beta cell destruction.
- Type 1b - non-autoimmune.
- Type 2 - insulin resistance with or without secretion defects.
- Gestational diabetes.

- Miscellaneous - endocrine, pancreatic, genetic, drug, chemical, or infection mediated.

Type 1 diabetes (insulin dependent - IDDM) is commonly seen in young people less than thirty years of age, with an average age of onset of 12–14 years. The disease is frequently autoimmune mediated. Onset is sudden, and the hallmark symptoms are weight loss, thirst, and fatigue. This type of diabetes is treated with insulin. *Type 2 diabetes* is genetically transmitted and is characterized by insulin resistance in the tissues. The hallmark symptom of this form of diabetes is weight gain, which has a slower onset compared with IDDM. Diet and exercise are nonpharmacological mainstays of treatment and oral diabetes agents are the drugs of choice used in Type 2 diabetes. Although usually thought of as a disease of adult onset, it is becoming more common in adolescents. Hallmark findings include severe obesity, hyperpigmentation, acanthosis nigricans (increased pigmentation and thickening of the skin of the posterior neck), and hypertension. Type 2 diabetes is more common in the African American and Mexican populations, in children, particularly girls, between the ages of 13–14, and in children with a family history of the disease. The most common oral agent utilized in pediatrics in the treatment of Type 2 diabetes is metformin (Glucophage®), although it does not have FDA approval for use in this population (Brosnan, Upchurch & Schreiver, 2001; Pinhas-Hamel & Zeitler, 2001).

Other oral agents that may be used include:

Alpha Glucosidase Inhibitors

Actions: delay absorption of carbohydrates.

Drugs in class: acarbose (Precose™)

Meglitinides

Actions: Stimulate insulin secretion from the pancreas.

Drugs in class: repoglinide (Prandin®)

Biguanides

Actions: Decrease glucose production and output from the liver, decreases intestinal glucose absorption and insulin sensitivity.

Drugs in class: Metformin (Glucophage)

Metformin - Glucophage

Pregnancy risk category: B

Contraindications: Sensitivity to the drug, renal or metabolic disease; temporarily withhold during radiologic studies using iodine contrast material due to risk of acute renal dysfunction.

Side Effects

Cardiovascular: Not significant.

Respiratory: Not significant.

GI-GU: Diarrhea, nausea, vomiting, abdominal bloating, anorexia.

Dermatological: Not significant.

Hematological: **Megaloblastic anemia, lactic acidosis.**

Neurological: Not significant.

Miscellaneous: None.

Food interactions: Alcohol potentiates effects.

Drug interactions: Calcium channel blockers, steroids, estrogens, oral contraceptives, phenytoin, diuretics, and thyroid drugs may produce hyperglycemia; drug levels may be increased in use with cimetidine, morphine, digoxin, ranitidine, trimethoprim, or vancomycin.

Insulin comes in many forms, based on duration of action.

- Fast-acting insulin, Humalog®, has a peak action of 1/2–1 hour, and lasts four to six hours.

- Short-acting insulin, regular or Semilente®, peaks at two to four hours and lasts six to eight hours.

- Intermediate insulin, NPH® or Lente®, peaks at 6–12 hours and lasts 16–24 hours.

- Long-acting insulin, ultralente, peaks at 16–18 hours and lasts up to 36 hours.

Premixed formulations of regular and NPH are available. If these two types of insulin need to be mixed from a multi-dose vial in the home, it is important to remember to draw up the *regular insulin* first. NPH insulin contains protamine, which could mix with regular insulin in the vial and inactivate it. The pregnancy risk for insulin is category B.

Patient teaching in insulin use:
- Monitor glucose and urine routinely.
- Meals and snacks should be taken consistently.
- Increase insulin dose with stress or during illness.
- Instruct in identification of hyperglycemia (thirst, frequent urination) and hypoglycemia (confusion, pallor, shakiness).
- Carry a glucose source for hypoglycemic episodes.

THYROID MEDICATIONS

The hypothalamic-pituitary-adrenal axis produces many hormones that are responsible for, among many other functions, the growth and development of secondary sexual characteristics. There is a feedback mechanism that occurs within this axis, responding to blood levels of free T4 or thyroid stimulating hormone (TSH). Production of free T4 in the thyroid sends a message to the hypothalamus to decrease production of thyroid regulating hormone (TRH), which in turn decreases production of TSH by the pituitary gland. In a state of *hyperthyroidism,* in which the defect occurs at the level of the thyroid gland, T4 would be abnormally elevated, and TRH and TSH levels correspondingly decreased. The opposite would be seen in *hypothyroidism.* Medications are administered to regulate the level of free T4 (Burns, Brady, Dunn & Starr, 2000; Wynne, Woo & Millard, 2002).

Thyroid Supplementation

Indications: Management of hypothyroidism.

Actions: Active component is T3; exact mechanism of action is unknown.

Drugs in class: Levothyroxine (Levoxyl®).

Levothyroxine - Levoxyl

Pregnancy risk category: A

Contraindications: Sensitivity to the drug or components, recent thyrotoxicosis, uncorrected adrenal insufficiency.

Side Effects

Cardiovascular: Tachycardia, palpitations, arrhythmias, angina, CHF, hypertension.

Respiratory: Not significant.

GI-GU: Diarrhea, abdominal cramps, increased appetite, weight loss.

Dermatological: Alopecia.

Hematological: Not significant.

Neurological: Tremors, insomnia, headache.

Miscellaneous: Diaphoresis.

Food interactions: Limit intake of cruciferous vegetables (broccoli, cabbage, etc.), soybean products decrease absorption.

Drug interactions: Iron salts, sucralfate, and antacids decrease absorption; increased metabolism of antidiabetic drugs; dose may need to be increased when taken with estrogens; drug may increase effects of anticoagulants.

Antithyroid Drugs

Indications: Management of hyperthyroidism.

Actions: Inhibit synthesis of thyroid hormones.

Drugs in class: Propothyouracil (PTU) - rapid onset of action, drug of choice in thyroid storm
methimazole (Tapazole®)

Methimazole (Tapazole)

Pregnancy risk category: D

Contraindications: Sensitivity to the drug or components, nursing mothers.

Side Effects

Cardiovascular: Edema, periarteritis.

Respiratory: Interstitial pneumonitis.

GI-GU: Nausea, vomiting, constipation, splenomegaly, weight gain.

Dermatological: Rash, urticaria, alopecia, skin pigmentation.

Hematological: **Agranulocytosis**, hypoprothrombinemia.

Neurological: Arthralgia, myalgia, neuritis, drowsiness, headache.

Miscellaneous: Goiter, nephritis, lupus like syndrome, lymphadenopathy, autoimmune syndrome, fever.

Food interactions: Not significant.

Drug interactions: Lithium and potassium iodide may potentiate effects; enhances effects of warfarin.

EXAM QUESTIONS

CHAPTER 3
Questions 21–29

21. The substance responsible for sodium regulation in the kidney is
    a. aldosterone.
    b. antidiuretic hormone.
    c. thyroxine.
    d. renin.

22. The strongest diuretic class is
    a. loop diuretics.
    b. potassium-sparing diuretics.
    c. osmotic diuretics.
    d. thiazide diuretics.

23. The class of diuretics that could cause gynecomastia in a young male patient is
    a. loop diuretics.
    b. potassium-sparing diuretics.
    c. osmotic diuretics.
    d. thiazide diuretics.

24. The pathophysiology behind GERD is
    a. structural defects with increased intra-abdominal pressure.
    b. increased lower esophageal sphincter (LES) tone and emptying time.
    c. decreased lower esophageal sphincter (LES) tone and delayed emptying time.
    d. mechanical obstruction and retrograde flow.

25. The effect of stimulation of the proton pump mechanism is
    a. stimulation of acetylcholine, gastrin, and histamine.
    b. neutralization of gastric acid.
    c. stimulation of H2 receptors.
    d. secretion of gastric acid.

26. GERD has been implicated in apnea in very young children due to
    a. decreased LES tone and mechanical obstruction.
    b. chemical irritation and increased gastric acidity.
    c. mechanical obstruction and chemical irritation.
    d. decreased gastric acidity and increased LES tone.

27. Drugs that may cause cardiac arrhythmias are
    a. H2 antagonists.
    b. prokinetics.
    c. leukotriene inhibitors.
    d. proton pump inhibitors.

28. When mixing NPH and regular insulins in the same syringe, an important point to keep in mind is

   a. *not* to mix these insulins in the same syringe.
   b. draw up the *regular* insulin first.
   c. draw up the *NPH* insulin first.
   d. first coat the inside of the syringe with protamine.

29. The caloric content of Polycose powder is 2 calories per teaspoon (tsp). The amount of Polycose to add to an ounce of formula or expressed breast milk to increase the caloric density by 4 calories per ounce would be

   a. 0.1 tsp.
   b. 1 tsp.
   c. 0.2 tsp.
   d. 2 tsp.

CHAPTER 4

ANTIBIOTICS AND VACCINES

CHAPTER OBJECTIVE

After completing this chapter, the reader will be able to specify the classifications of vaccines and antibiotic medications and indicate the applicable nursing implications for the administration of these drugs.

LEARNING OBJECTIVES

At the completion of the chapter, the reader will be able to:

1. recognize which vaccines and antibiotic medications are commonly used in the pediatric population.
2. specify common conditions in the pediatric population which may benefit from the administration of these medications.
3. recognize common side effects of the use of these medications.

THE IMMUNE RESPONSE

The immune system is responsible for providing immediate and long term defense against infective organisms. On exposure to an infective agent, a cascade is initiated in which lymphocytes are activated, then migrate, adhere to, and digest the organism (chemotaxis and phagocytosis). The thymus gland is important in the process, so this is called *T cell or cell-mediated immunity*. Other lymphocyte cell types called B cells, found in the liver prenatally and in the bone marrow in later life, produce immunoglobulins, which are designed to recognize specific antigens and bind to their receptor sites, marking them as invaders to be destroyed by killer cells. This process is termed B cell immunity. These mechanisms are supported by natural protective mechanisms such as the skin, stomach acid, and the complement cascade.

The very young child is particularly susceptible to infections for several reasons. These children have decreased circulating levels of fibronectin and complement as well as a low neutrophil pool that is not only rapidly depleted but also ineffectively mobilized to fight infection. There is a sluggish response of stem cells to form white cell lines and a low volume of immunoglobulins. Infants receive immunoglobulins transplacentally from their mothers that provide postnatal immunity for about six months; however, this immunity is only conferred for those organisms to which the mother was exposed. The maternally acquired immunoglobulins may not be specific to the infective agents with which the newborn comes into contact.

Immunoglobulins (Ig) are produced by B cells, so named because they were first found in the bursa (joints) of birds. There are five classifications of immunoglobulins:

1. IgA and secretory IgA - provide protection to mucous membranes of the respiratory and GI tracts.
2. IgD - thought to facilitate the development of lymphocyte antigen receptor sites.
3. IgE - involved in allergic reactions.
4. IgM - an immunoglobulin produced by the newborn.
5. IgG - the only immunoglobulin to cross the placenta; after about thirty six weeks of gestation provides the fetus and the newborn with maternally acquired immunity.

Infections can be transmitted to the pediatric patient in many ways, including airborne droplets, ingestion of contaminated food or water, direct contact, and in the fetus by vaginal or transplacental transmission. During an infection, certain white cell lines may be altered and can be measured in a white blood count (WBC). Early in infection, the white blood cell components are mobilized to fight the infection, so the WBC rises. The longer the duration or the more severe the infection, the fewer WBCs are available, so the WBC count may fall and immature white cell types rise; this is called a *left shift*. If the white cell lines are pictured as developing in a left to right linear fashion, the less mature types would be on the left side of the line and the more mature cell types on the right. So the younger the cells seen, the more to the left, or left shifted, the WBC count is said to be (Blumer, 2001; Pickering, 2000).

Example: myelocyte → metamyelocyte → band → granulocyte (also called PMN)

immature WBCs → mature WBCs

Bacterial and viral cells require nutrients to form, and many antibiotics and antivirals interfere with nutrient acquisition or with cell wall formation. Antibiotics are chosen based on the *type and sensitivity* of the organism, *patient factors* such as liver and kidney function (elimination and drug levels), age, *immune system function* (sensitivity of the patient to side effects of the drug), *efficacy, safety, and cost* of the drug. Some medications are contraindicated for use in specific populations: Metronidazole (Flagyl®), chloramphenicol, and antineoplastics during pregnancy, or fluoroquinolones, which are used with caution in children as they can damage joints, particularly during periods of rapid growth.

Narrow spectrum antibiotics are used for specific, sensitive organisms, e.g., vancomycin for methicillin-resistant *staphylococcus aureus* (MRSA). *Broad spectrum* drugs such as chloramphenicol and tetracycline are used against both gram-positive and gram-negative organisms. Drugs are often *combined* to provide broad spectrum coverage prior to identification of an organism and its sensitivity and to prevent antibiotic resistance. A combination of ampicillin and gentamicin is an example.

Drug resistance is becoming an increasing problem in the treatment of infection, as more and stronger drugs are given. Organisms develop resistance in several ways: by spontaneous mutation of the organism, alteration of drug receptor sites, development of decreased membrane permeability to a drug, or by enzyme inactivation of drug. Antibiotic resistance can be minimized with the following approaches:

- When a medication is prescribed, it should be used for the entire length of time recommended.
- Unused portions of antibiotics should not be shared.
- Use of antimicrobial hand washes should be minimized.
- Antibiotics should be used only when indicated—a viral illness is best treated symptomatically.
- Adverse effects should be reported immediately.

- When children are receiving immunizations they may be pretreated with acetaminophen or ibuprofen for fever and discomfort.

In October of 2000, a new classification of antibiotic was introduced, called *oxazolidinones*. This classification of drug was developed to treat resistant gram-positive organisms such as methicillin-resistant *staphylococcus aureus* (MRSA) and vancomycin-resistant entercocci (VRE). The one drug in the class is linezolid (Zyvox™). This drug acts by interfering with bacterial production earlier in the process than do other antibiotics. Side effects include gastrointestinal symptoms and decreased platelets. It will be interesting to follow the progress of this new classification of antibiotic (Wynne, Woo & Millard, 2002; Young, 2000).

VACCINES

Vaccines and immunoglobulins provide either active or passive resistance against specific organisms. There are four types of vaccines: *attenuated*, or weakened, virus such as IPV, MMR, and varicella; *killed* virus such as pertussis and influenza; bacterial or viral *toxoids* (antigens) such as diphtheria and tetanus, and *synthetic* vaccines such as HiB. Live or attenuated vaccines stimulate an immune response that may last years before the immunoglobulins developed begin to wane. Vaccines developed from killed organisms do not generate as intense an immune response. Passive resistance is conferred by the administration of immunoglobulins of the IgG class, which are given to facilitate killing of or immunity to multiple infective organisms. These immunoglobulins are harvested from a pool of donors who have been exposed and developed immunity to various specific organisms. Because individual immune responses vary, the effectiveness of immunoglobulins may also be variable.

Frequently the question arises whether to immunize preterm infants based on postnatal or postconceptual age. In general, there is no contraindication to immunizing these children at the appropriate *postnatal* age, with the exception of the hepatitis vaccine, the first dose of which is given after the child reaches two kilograms in weight. Immunization guidelines may be downloaded from the CDC website: http://www.cdc.gov.

Prior to administration of a vaccine, informed consent must be obtained. A legal guardian or parent may sign, and they must be given information on benefits and risks. VIS (vaccine information sheets) are available from the CDC or from local departments of public health. Consent, date and time of administration, manufacturer and lot of vaccine, signature of administrator, as well as any adverse reactions experienced must be documented. Adverse reactions are documented and sent to local public health departments utilizing a VAERS (*Vaccine Adverse Event Reporting System*) form (Lieberman, 2001; Pickering, 2000; Shields, 2001; Waldrop, 2001).

General Vaccination Considerations

- Vaccines must be refrigerated at 35–45 degrees F.
- Refrigerator temperature must be maintained and documented.
- Varicella vaccine is stored at 5 degrees F.
- Live vaccines are given SQ (varicella, IPV, MMR)*.
- Inactive vaccines are given IM (all others).
- If giving more than one vaccine, they are given in separate sites and separate syringes.
- Administration of blood products, particularly gamma globulins, may decrease response to vaccines.
- Adverse reactions may include redness, pain at the injection site, low-grade fever.
- Severe reactions include prolonged crying, lethargy, and seizure activity.

- 1:1000 epinephrine must be kept on hand for anaphylactic reactions.

General Contraindications

- Previous reaction to vaccine or components.
- Moderate to severe current illness with or without fever.
- Live vaccines should not be given within one month of each other.
- Live virus vaccines should not be given within 3–6 months of the patient receiving immunoglobulin therapy.

Vaccination is not Contraindicated in

- Mild to moderate current illness with or without fever.
- Local reaction after previous vaccination.
- Receiving antibiotics.
- Prematurity (but see hepatitis B vaccine).
- Exposure to infectious disease.
- Breastfeeding.
- History of allergies.

Hepatitis B

The illness: Hepatitis B is a hepadnavirus. The family of hepadnaviruses includes:

Hepatitis A - spread by the fecal-oral route.

Hepatitis B - spread by blood and body fluids.

Hepatitis C - spread parenterally, no immunization available.

Hepatitis D - concurrent with hepatitis B, no immunization available.

Hepatitis E - spread by the fecal-oral route. This disease is rare in the United States and no immunization is available.

Hepatitis G - seen in organ transplant patients. This disease may be asymptomatic or mild and may be protective against HIV; no immunization is available.

It is helpful to know what the following laboratory findings indicate:

HbsAg - surface antigen, indicates acute illness.

HbsAb - surface antibody, indicates resolving illness.

HbeAg - core antigen, indicates acute illness.

HbeAb - core antibody, indicates resolving illness.

HbcAg - core antigen, indicates chronic illness.

Type of vaccine: The hepatitis B vaccine is synthetic, recombinant.

Given: Given to infants weighing 2000 grams or more; delay until 2 months of age if infant weighs less than 2000 grams.

Contraindications: History of anaphylaxis to baker's yeast.

***Not* contraindicated in:** Pregnancy, breastfeeding.

Other considerations:

Recommended for high risk groups such as
- health care workers;
- residents of group homes;
- contacts of those with chronic HBV; and
- those living or traveling in areas where the virus is endemic.

Current controversies include

- thimerosal component removed; and
- two European studies claimed a relationship between the vaccine and exacerbation or causation of multiple sclerosis—this has been disproved.

Hepatitis A

The illness: A picornavirus, common in children 5–14 years of age.

How spread: Fecal-oral route.

How treated: Supportive treatment.

Type of vaccine: Inactive.

Contraindications: Active neurological problems.

Not **contraindicated in:** Pregnancy or breastfeeding.

Other considerations: Recommended for high risk groups including

- children older than two years living in areas with high rates;
- Alaskan, Native American, Pacific Islanders;
- those with hemophiliac or chronic liver disease;
- food handlers; and
- those living in areas of periodic or current outbreaks.

HIB (Haemophilus Influenza B)

The illness: *Haemophilus influenzae*, a gram-negative coccobacillus, causes acute otitis media, sinusitis, conjunctivitis, pneumonia, and meningitis in children.

How spread: Person to person, droplet.

How treated: Amoxicillin-clavulanate (Augmentin®).

Type of vaccine: Synthetic.

Contraindications: See general contraindications.

Not **contraindicated in:** Previous history of H flu illness, pregnancy, breastfeeding.

Other considerations: Before vaccination, HIB was the number one cause of meningitis in children.

DTaP (Diphtheria, Tetanus, and Pertussis)

The Illness

Diphtheria - a gram-positive bacillus, causing membranous pharyngitis and upper respiratory secretions; spread by droplet and person to person contact; treated with erythromycin or benzathine penicillin.

Pertussis - a gram-negative bacillus, spread by droplet and person to person, treated with erythromycin, clarithromycin or co-trimoxazole (TMP-SMX).

Tetanus - an anaerobic gram-positive bacillus, spread by contaminated wounds, treated with the toxoid and gamma globulin.

Type of vaccine: DT - toxoid, aP - killed virus.

Contraindications: Positive history of pertussis, encephalopathy within seven days of vaccination, after the age of seven years Td is given.

Not **contraindicated in:** Pregnancy or breastfeeding.

Other considerations: The DTP vaccine contained whole cells, which caused reactions. DTaP contains agglutinated (fragmented) cells, which reduces the occurrence of side effects.

IPV (Inactivated Polio Virus)

The illness: An enterovirus.

How spread: Fecal-oral and oral-oral routes.

How treated: Supportive.

Type of vaccine: Attenuated live.

Contraindications: Reactions to streptomycin, polymyxin B, neomycin.

Not contraindicated in: Pregnancy or breastfeeding.

Other considerations: The oral formulation provides gut protection but is shed in excreta and presents a risk to immunocompromised family members. Because of this, the injectable formulation has been recommended since 2000 as the only formulation of polio vaccine given to immunocompromised patients and household contacts. Special circumstances when OPV would be given include imminent travel to an area where polio is endemic, catch-up immunization, or parental refusal of the injectable form.

MMR (Measles, Mumps, Rubella)

The Illness

Measles - a paramyxovirus, spread by the airborne route, treated with ribaviran and vitamin A to minimize the severity of symptoms, treated symptomatically.

Mumps - a paramyxovirus, droplet spread, treated symptomatically.

Rubella - a rubivirus, nasopharyngeal droplet spread, treated symptomatically.

Type of vaccine: Attenuated live virus.

Contraindications: Pregnancy, and avoid pregnancy for three months after immunization, immunocompromised patients or patients with hemophiliac diseases, high dose steroid therapy, anaphylactic reaction to gelatin or neomycin.

Not **contraindicated in:** Breastfeeding, non-anaphylactic reactions to gelatin or neomycin.

Other considerations: Radiation, administration of IgG may decrease response.

Current controversies: Some studies have found a relationship between MMR vaccine and autism and irritable bowel disease. This relationship has not been proven; the time from vaccination to onset of illness was identified as being between 1–9 years.

Varicella

The illness: A herpesvirus.

How spread: Person to person, droplets.

How treated: Acyclovir, varicella immunoglobulin (VZIG) after exposure.

Type of vaccine: Attenuated live virus.

Contraindications: Reactions to neomycin or gelatin products, pregnancy, active varicella or zoster disease within 21 days of immunization, immunocompromised individuals, high dose steroid therapy.

Not **contraindicated in:** Breastfeeding.

Other considerations: Must be frozen, used within 30 minutes then discarded, provides immunity to zoster as well, which can become dormant, so vaccine may result in shingles.

Pneumococcal Vaccine

The illness: *Streptococcus pneumoniae,* a gram-positive diplococcus, most common cause of acute otitis media (AOM) and sinusitis in children.

How spread: Rspiratory droplet contact.

How treated: Amoxicillin, amoxicillin-clavulanate (Augmentin) for resistant *S. pneumoniae*.

Type of vaccine: Synthetic.

Contraindications: Sensitivity to the vaccine or to thimerosal.

Not **contraindicated in:** Pregnancy or breastfeeding if the patient is considered high risk for the illness.

Other considerations: There are two formulations, a 23 valent formulation that is not recommended for children less than 2 years of age due to their limited ability to mount an immune response to the immunization, and a newer 7 valent formulation that is used in children older than 2 months.

Recommended in certain high risk groups: Children with sickle cell disease, asplenia, chronic renal failure, immunosuppressed conditions, HIV, and cerebrospinal fluid leaks.

Meningococcal Vaccine

The illness: *Neisseria meningitidis,* a gram-negative diplococcus.

How spread: Person to person.

How treated: Rifampin, ceftriaxone, ciprofloxacin or sulfisoxazole if resistant.

Type of vaccine: Synthetic.

Contraindications: Reaction to thimerosal, infants less than 2 years of age.

Not **contraindicated in:** Pregnancy or breastfeeding.

Other considerations: Recommended for high risk groups including: asplenic, immunocompromised patients, military recruits, or children in group settings such as group homes or college dormitories, those exposed to outbreaks, those with sickle cell disease or HIV.

Other Vaccines

RSV (Respiratory Syncytial Virus)

The illness: A paramyxovirus, common cause of bronchiolitis in infants.

How spread: Droplets or secretions.

How treated: Antivirals.

Type of vaccine: RespiGam is a monoclonal antibody, given to newborns at high risk of developing respiratory syncytial virus.

Given: Once a month for the duration of the RSV season (late fall to spring).

Contraindications: Severe cardiac illness, reaction to drug or components.

Rotavirus - no longer on the market due to association with intussusception in infants.

Lyme (Lymerix)

The illness: *Borrelia burgdorferi,* a bacterial spirochete.

How spread: Tick borne.

How treated: Doxycycline or ceftriaxone.

Type: Synthetic.

Given: Ages 15–70 years, three doses, given at 1 and 12 months following first dose to susceptible populations several weeks before Lyme season.

Contraindications: Those outside age range, sensitivity to drug or components, antibiotic resistant Lyme.

Other considerations: Developed in 1998, antibody is active against *B. burgdorferi spirochete* while tick is attached to host, attacks spirochete in tick's midsection. The vaccine has recently been withdrawn from the market due to low demand.

Influenza

The illness: three types of virus—A, B, and C. The virus constantly changes from outbreak to outbreak.

How spread: Droplet, person to person.

How treated: Amantidine/rimantidine given within 48 hours of disease diminishes severity of symptoms, other antivirals include zanamivir, oseltamivir.

Type: Killed virus.

Contraindications: Egg or thimerosal sensitivity, not given within three days of DTaP vaccination.

ANTIBIOTICS

Folate Antagonists/Inhibitors of Folate Reduction

Action: Inhibit organisms from synthesizing folic acid.

Indications: Gram-negative enteric organisms, burns, urinary tract infections, but not for use in group A *beta hemolytic streptococcal* infections.

Side effects: Crystalluria and folate deficiency.

Drugs in class: Sulfamethoxazole (Gantanol®)
　　　　trimethoprim (Proloprim®)
　　　　trimethoprim - sulfamethoxazole (Cotrim®, Bactrim®)

Trimethoprim - Sulfamethoxazole (Cotrim, Bactrim)

Pregnancy risk category: C

Contraindications: Sensitivity to the drug or components, porphyria, folate deficiency anemia, infants less than two months of age.

Side Effects

　　Cardiovascular: Not significant.

Respiratory: Not significant.

GI-GU: Nausea, vomiting, diarrhea, stomatitis.

Dermatological: Rash, **erythema multiforme, Stevens-Johnson syndrome.**

Hematological: **Thrombocytopenia, agranulocytosis, aplastic anemia,** leukopenia, hemolysis in G6PD.

Neurological: **Seizures**, confusion, depression, ataxia, headache.

Miscellaneous: **Serum sickness, necrotizing hepatitis, anaphylaxis.**

Food interactions: Not significant.

Drug interactions: Decreases clearance of warfarin, increases effects of phenobarbital, decreases cyclosporin levels, decreases effectiveness of oral contraceptives.

Drugs That Inhibit Cell Wall Synthesis

These drugs include penicillins and cephalosporins. The penicillin family is divided into two groups of medications, the beta lactams and the beta lactamase inhibitors. Beta lactam penicillins contain a chemical bond that resistant organisms are able to disrupt through an enzyme called beta lactamase. Beta lactamase inhibitors prevent the production of this enzyme in the organism's cell wall and thus prevent resistance.

Indications: Gram-positive and gram-negative organisms, skin, joint infections and urinary tract infections.

Side effects: Hypersensitivity or resistance, rash, anemia, pseudomembranous colitis.

Drugs in class: beta lactams and beta lactamase inhibitors.
- vancomycin (Vancocin®)
- beta lactams - penicillins
- beta lactamase resistant drugs -
  - cloxacillin (Tegopen®)
  - dicloxacillin (Dynapen®)
  - nafcillin (Nafcil®)
  - methicillin (Unipen®)
  - oxacillin (Prostaphilin®)
- cephalosporins -
  - First generation—indicated for burns and skin infections, have minimal CNS penetration.
    - cefadroxil (Duricef®)
    - cefazolin (Ancef®)
    - cephalexin (Keflex®)
    - cephalothin (Keflin®)
  - Second generation—also have poor CNS penetration.
    - cefaclor (Ceclor®)
    - cefamandol (Mandol®)
    - cefotetan (Cefotan®)
    - cefoxitin (Mefoxin®)
    - cefprozil (Cefzil®)
    - cefuroxime (Ceftin®)
  - Third generation—indicated for H flu, E coli, otitis, better CNS penetration.
    - cefixime (Suprax®)
    - cefotaxime (Claforan®)
    - cefpodoxime (Vantin®)
    - ceftazidine (Fortaz®)
    - ceftriaxone (Rocephin®)

Ceftriaxone (Rocephin)

Pregnancy risk category: B

Contraindications: Sensitivity to the drug or other cephalosporins.

Side Effects

Cardiovascular: Not significant.

Respiratory: Not significant.

GI-GU: nausea, Vomiting, diarrhea, **pseudomembranous colitis,** vaginitis.

Dermatological: Phlebitis, rash.

Hematological: Elevated BUN, eosinophilia, **leukopenia.**

Neurological: Headache, dizziness.

Miscellaneous: Anaphylaxis, kernicterus in

premature infants.

Food interactions: Not significant.

Drug interactions: Not significant.

Drugs That Inhibit Protein Synthesis

Indications: Aerobic organisms, acne.

Side effects: Blood dyscrasias, stained teeth, photosensitivity, decrease absorption of calcium, magnesium, and aluminum.

Drugs in class: tetracycline (Vibramycin®)
   aminoglycosides
      amikacin (Amikin®)
      gentamicin (Ganamycin®)
      kanamicin (Kantrex®)
      neomycin (Neocin®)
   macrolides
      azithromycin (Zithromax®)
      erythromycin
      clarithromycin (Biaxin®)
   chloramphenicol (Chloromycetin®)
   clindamycin (Cleocin®)

Gentamicin

Pregnancy risk category: D

Contraindications: Sensitivity to the drug or components.

Side Effects

   Cardiovascular: Hypotension.

   Respiratory: **Apnea.**

   GI-GU: Nausea and vomiting, **nephrotoxicity**.

   Dermatological: Pruritis, rash.

   Hematological: **Aagranulocytosis, thrombocytosis, leukopenia,** eosinophilia, hypomagnesemia.

   Neurological: Dizziness, ataxia, headache, seizures.

   Miscellaneous: **Ototoxicity**, tinnitus.

Food interactions: Not significant.

Drug interactions: Cephalosporins, loop diuretics, vancomycin, and indomethacin increase toxicity.

Azithromycin (Zithromax)

Pregnancy risk category: B

Contraindications: Sensitivity to macrolide antibiotics.

Side Effects

   Cardiovascular: Palpitations, chest pain.

   Respiratory: Not significant.

   GI-GU: Nnausea, vomiting, diarrhea, abdominal pain, vaginitis, melena.

   Dermatological: Rash, pruritis, photosensitivity, candidal infections, **Stevens-Johnson syndrome.**

   Hematological: Eelevated liver enzymes, jaundice.

   Neurological: Headache, dizziness, agitation, insomnia.

   Miscellaneous: **Anaphylaxis, ototoxicity.**

Food interactions: Ingestion with food decreases bioavailability.

Drug interactions: Antacids decrease serum levels.

Drugs That Inhibit Nucleic Acid Function

Indications: Urinary tract infections, tuberculosis, fungal infections.

Side effects: Articular cartilage erosion (joint damage) in children younger than 18 years.

Drugs in class: fluoroquinolones - ciprofloxacin (Cipro®)
      ofloxacin (Floxin®)
      norfloxacin (Noroxin®)
      levofloxacin (Levaquin®) -
   this is a long acting drug and is a P-450 inhibitor.
   antimycobacterials - isoniazid (INH)
      rifampin (Rifadin®)
   antifungals - tolnaftate (Tinactin®)
      nystatin (Mycostatin®)
      clotrimazole (Mycelex®)

ketoconazole (Nizoral®)
griseofulvin (Fulvicin®)

Ciprofloxacin (Cipro)

Pregnancy risk category: C

Contraindications: Sensitivity to the drug or other fluoroquinolones, not used systemically in children under 18 years of age.

Side Effects

    Cardiovascular: None significant.

    Respiratory: None significant.

    GI-GU: Nausea, diarrhea, vomiting, abdominal pain, **pseudomembranous colitis.**

    Dermatological: Rash, photosensitivity, pruritis, urticaria, **Stevens-Johnson syndrome, toxic epidermal necrolysis.**

    Hematological: Anemia, eosinophilia, **neutropenia, leukopenia.**

    Neurological: Headache, restlessness, tremor, dizziness, insomnia, seizures.

    Miscellaneous: Crystalluria, elevated liver enzymes, articular erosion in children under 18 years of age.

Food interactions: Food delays absorption, caffeine effects increased.

Drug interactions: Antacids, iron containing vitamins, and sucralfate decrease absorption, Cipro decreased metabolism of theophylline.

Nystatin (Mycostatin)

Pregnancy risk category: B

Contraindications: Hypersensitivity to drug or components.

Side Effects

    Cardiovascular: Not significant.

    Respiratory: Not significant.

    GI-GU: Nausea, vomiting, diarrhea with oral solution.

    Dermatological: Contact dermatitis, **Stevens-Johnson syndrome.**

    Hematological: Not significant.

    Neurological: Not significant.

    Miscellaneous: Not significant.

Food interactions: Not significant.

Drug interactions: Not significant.

EXAM QUESTIONS

CHAPTER 4
Questions 30–39

30. A term used to describe WBC response to infection is

    a. cell-mediated immunity.
    b. natural protective defense.
    c. complement cascade.
    d. B cell immunity.

31. The term "left shift" when applied to the WBC count means

    a. an increase in circulating mature white blood cells.
    b. a decrease in circulating immature white cells.
    c. a decrease in circulating mature white cells.
    d. an increase in circulating immature white cells.

32. One mechanism for the development of antibiotic resistance is

    a. alteration of receptor sites.
    b. enzyme activation.
    c. increased membrane permeability.
    d. combination therapy.

33. An immune response is elicited by administration of

    a. immunoglobulins.
    b. organism-specific IgG.
    c. attenuated vaccine.
    d. fibronectin.

34. A common contraindication for administration of vaccines to a child is

    a. mild to moderate illness with a fever.
    b. previous reaction to a vaccine or component.
    c. concurrent antibiotic therapy.
    d. local reaction.

35. The one common childhood vaccine with a weight restriction for administration is

    a. hepatitis immunoglobulin.
    b. HIB vaccine.
    c. Respigam.
    d. hepatitis B vaccine.

36. Organism resistance to penicillin class antibiotics is due to the presence of

    a. beta lactamase.
    b. fibronectin.
    c. complement.
    d. passive resistance.

37. An antibiotic class which should be used with caution in growing pediatric patients due to joint damage is

    a. macrolides.
    b. fluoroquinolones.
    c. aminoglycosides.
    d. cephalosporins.

38. An ampicillin vial contains 250 mg and is diluted to 100 mg per ml. To administer a dose of 125 mg, you would draw up

    a. 0.5 ml.

    b. 1.25 ml.

    c. 075 ml.

    d. 2.5 ml.

39. A cutaneous side effect of certain antibiotics is

    a. thrombocytopenia.

    b. erythema multiforme.

    c. pseudomembranous colitis.

    d. ataxia.

CHAPTER 5

NEUROLOGICAL MEDICATIONS

CHAPTER OBJECTIVE

After completing this chapter, the reader will be able to specify the classifications of neurological and pain medications and indicate the applicable nursing implications for the administration of these drugs.

LEARNING OBJECTIVES

At the completion of the chapter, the reader will be able to

1. recognize which neurological and pain medications are commonly used in the pediatric population.
2. specify common conditions in the pediatric population that may benefit from the administration of these medications.
3. recognize common side effects of the use of these medications.

PAIN MEDICATIONS

The sensation of pain is stimulated by release of inflammatory mediators such as prostaglandins, leukotrienes, and histamine. Pain receptors, also called nociceptors, respond to this stimulus by sending a signal to the spinal cord through either fast-conducting A fibers, (acute, localized, sharp pain sensation) or slow-conducting C fibers (chronic, dull, diffuse, persistent pain). The message is transmitted to the CNS where it is processed, and the message sent to peripheral nerves. Peripherally myelinized nerve fibers comprise about 20% of nerve fibers in adults; they are responsible for sharp, stinging pain sensation. Unmyelinized fibers are responsible for dull, throbbing pain sensation. Myelinization is complete in the newborn at about 36–37 weeks gestation. Prior to this time unmyelinized nerves conduct pain impulses more slowly, but this is offset by the smaller size of the baby and shorter distances for the impulse to travel.

The assessment of pain can be difficult in children, particularly in preverbal or nonverbal children. Physiological responses that indicate pain include changes in heart rate, respiratory rate, blood pressure, oxygenation, activity level, and responsiveness, although very young children may become habituated to noxious and painful stimuli and respond more subtly. Behavioral indicators include vocalizations, changes in sleep patterns or body posture, facial expressions, guarding or avoidance of the painful area, and other changes in behavior such as avoidance of interaction or anger. There are many pain rating scales available which may be used to assess the severity of pain, and along with a pain history (OLDCHART mnemonic - Onset, Location, Duration, Characteristics, Aggravating factors, Relief methods, Treatments sought) may be helpful in identifying nonpharmacological as well as pharmacological therapies.

Since pain perception and tolerance are so individualized, the keys to management of pain are to maintain scheduled pain medication dosages and supplement with PRN doses. Nonpharmacologic pain relief methods are also maximized and are based on the gateway theory of pain perception. This theory postulates that pain perception is intensified by anticipation or agitation and may be blocked by breathing and relaxation techniques or by touch. In addition, pain may be controlled by an endogenous pain control pathway that can be enhanced with nonpharmacological pain relief methods.

Nonpharmacologic methods that may be helpful in newborns include swaddling, non-nutritive sucking, position changes, administration of glucose water, cuddling, and minimal stimulation. In older children, relaxation techniques, play or music therapy, application of heat or cold, massage, acupuncture or rest, and immobilization should be used in conjunction with pharmacological pain relief that includes non-steroidal anti-inflammatories (NSAIDs) and narcotic medications (Harvey & Champe, 1997; Heubi, 1999; Lynn, Ulma & Spieker, 1999).

NSAIDS

Action: Inhibit prostaglandin synthesis by inhibiting cyclo-oxygenase enzyme (COX enzyme).

Indications: Inflammation, pain, and fever.

Drugs in class: Salicylates - ASA - contraindicated in children except in the treatment of Kawasaki's disease and juvenile arthritis due to the risk of Reye's syndrome (liver and neurological damage).

Propionic acids - ibuprofen (Motrin®) and naproxen (Naprosyn®).

Acetic acids - indomethacin (Indocin®), ketorolac (Toradol®). Ketorolac has recently been investigated for IV use in infants less than one year old for pain relief. It has a low side effect profile; however, hypovolemia should be corrected prior to administration, due to possible hypotension.

COX 2 inhibitors - Celebrex™ - selectively inhibit COX 2 receptor sites, but not COX 1 sites, stimulation of which results in GI irritation.

Ibuprofen (Motrin)

Pregnancy risk category: B, D in third trimester

Contraindications: Hypersensitivity to the drug, components or other NSAIDs, patients with GI bleeding or ulcers, decreased renal function, hypertension. Maximum dose should not exceed 3.2 grams per day.

Side Effects

Cardiovascular: None significant.

Respiratory: None significant.

GI-GU: Nausea, vomiting, abdominal pain, **GI bleed and perforation.**

Dermatological: Rash, urticaria.

Hematological: **Neutropenia, anemia, agranulocytosis.**

Neurological: Dizziness, drowsiness, fatigue, headache.

Miscellaneous: Hepatitis, tinnitus, vision changes, renal failure.

Food interactions: Food decreases the rate of absorption.

Drug interactions: Increases digoxin, methotrexate, and lithium concentrations; decreases effects of diuretics; other GI irritants may increase GI side effects; aspirin decreases concentrations.

Non-Narcotic Analgesics

Action: Inhibit prostaglandin synthesis.

Indications: Mild pain and fever, but not inflammation.

Drugs in class: Acetaminophen (Tylenol®).

Acetaminophen (Tylenol)

Pregnancy risk category: B

Contraindications: Sensitivity to the drug or components.

Side Effects

Cardiovascular: Not significant.

Respiratory: Not significant.

GI-GU: Hepatic necrosis with overdose greater than 4 grams per day, renal injury with chronic use.

Dermatological: Rash.

Hematological: Neutropenia, leukopenia.

Neurological: Not significant.

Miscellaneous: Hypersensitivity reactions. The risk of overdose in children is increased because of the many formulations—children may be overdosed by any of the following ways:

- *Drops* (80 mg/ml) given at the same dose as the liquid formulation (160 mg/5 ml).
- *Adult tablets* (325 mg) given rather than children's tablets (160 mg).
- *Tylenol* given with cold preparations that contain Tylenol.

Food interactions: Food decreases rate of absorption.

Drug interactions: Enzyme inhibitors and alcohol increase hepatic damage.

Narcotics/Opiates

Narcotics bind to opiate receptor sites to suppress pain. There are four receptor sites:

1. mu - μ in the CNS - stimulation produces analgesia and respiratory depression.
2. delta - δ in the limbic area - stimulation produces euphoria.
3. kappa - κ in the cortex - stimulation produces sedation.
4. sigma - σ in the ANS - stimulation produces hallucinations.

Opiates may be classified as *agonists,* in which stimulation of the receptor site produces the above mentioned responses; *partial agonists*, in which only a partial response is produced; or *antagonists,* which inhibit the response when the receptor is stimulated. Antagonists are used to reverse narcotic effects. Side effects of overdose of these medications may include euphoria, sedation, pinpoint pupils (miosis), respiratory depression, nausea and vomiting, urinary retention, and itching secondary to histamine release.

Agonists

morphine

hydromorphone (Dilaudid®)

methadone (Dolopine®)

meperidine (Demerol®)

fentanyl (Sublimaze®)

oxycodone (Percocet®, Percodan®)

propoxyphene (Darvon®)

Partial Agonists

Drugs in class: nalbuphine (Nubain®)
butrophanol (Stadol®)

Antagonists

Side Effects: Short duration of action, so effects of narcotic may return. In drug-addicted patients, use of antagonists may stimulate seizure from rapid withdrawal.

Drugs in class: Naloxone (Narcan®)

Fentanyl (Sublimaze)

Pregnancy risk category: C, D if used at high doses at term, or for prolonged periods.

Contraindications: Sensitivity to the drug or components, patients taking MAO inhibitors.

Side Effects

Cardiovascular: Palpitations, hyper- or

hypotension, arrhythmias.

Respiratory: **Respiratory depression, apnea.**

GI-GU: Nausea, vomiting, constipation or diarrhea, urinary retention, abdominal pain, dry mouth, anorexia.

Dermatological: Pruritis, diaphoresis.

Hematological: Not significant.

Neurological: CNS depression, dizziness, drowsiness, headache, anxiety, depression.

Miscellaneous: Dependence, histamine release, irritation at site of injection

Food interactions: Not significant.

Drug interactions: Additive effects when used with CNS depressants, alcohol, narcotic analgesics, TCAs, and MAOIs.

Naloxone (Narcan)

Pregnancy risk category: B

Contraindications: Sensitivity to drug or components.

Side Effects

Cardiovascular: Hypertension or hypotension, tachycardia, **ventricular arrhythmia, cardiac arrest.**

Respiratory: Not significant.

GI-GU: Nausea, vomiting.

Dermatological: Not significant.

Hematological: Not significant.

Neurological: Not significant.

Miscellaneous: Diaphoresis, may cause withdrawal in newborns of narcotic dependent mothers.

Food interactions: Not significant.

Drug interactions: Not significant.

Additional medications that may be used in pain control include:

TCAs and antidepressants (*see* Psychiatric drug section), which are used on neuropathic (phantom limb) pain, steroids that are used in inflammation-induced pain and increased intracranial pressure, and benzodiazepines, used in muscular pain or spasm.

Emla is a lidocaine-prilocaine-containing topical analgesic cream that is used to prevent pain from injections. It comes as a small occlusive dressing that is placed over the site of injection for about thirty minutes prior to administration. Methemoglobinemia is a rare side effect seen in the use of this drug.

HEADACHE

Headaches occur commonly in children and may be vascular (migraines), muscular (tension), or inflammatory (intracranial) in origin. Migraine headaches are usually preceded by an aura and are characterized by unilateral throbbing pain. Tension headaches are characterized by dull occipital or frontal pain. Therapy involves pain management and interruptive or prophylactic therapy for migraines that interfere with activities. Acetaminophen and ibuprofen are the drugs of choice for pain management. Other medications include selective serotonin reuptake inhibitors (Imitrex®), tricyclic antidepressants (amitryptyline, nortriptyline) (*see* Psychiatric Drug Section for a discussion of these drugs), and ergot alkaloids (ergotamine) that act by constricting cerebral vasculature (Burns, Brady, Dunn & Starr, 2000; Wynne, Woo & Millard, 2002).

Ergotamine

Pregnancy risk category: X

Contraindications: Sensitivity to the drug, to caffeine, or any component, peripheral vascular disease, liver or renal disease, sepsis, coronary artery disease.

Side Effects

Cardiovascular: Precordial pain, vasospasm or constriction, claudication, transient bradycardia or tachycardia.

Respiratory: Not significant.

GI-GU: Nausea, vomiting, diarrhea, dry mouth.

Dermatological: Pruritus.

Hematological: Not significant.

Neurological: Weakness.

Miscellaneous: Myalgia, edema, leg cramps.

Food interactions: Caffeine increases absorption.

Drug interactions: Peripheral vasoconstriction enhanced with macrolides, beta blockers.

PSYCHIATRIC DRUGS

Depression is a pervasive condition, characterized by changes in mood, appetite, sleep, and behavior. Pediatric patients manifest depression differently than do adults; whereas adults demonstrate depressed mood or decreased pleasure in activities, in the pediatric patient depression is manifested by feelings of powerlessness and pessimism. Irritability and agitation may also be noted in children. Children at high risk of developing depression include those with poor socioeconomic status, residents of rural areas, and children with a family history of depression.

The pathophysiology of depression is alteration of the CNS neurotransmitters dopamine, serotonin, and norepinephrine. Antidepressants inhibit reuptake of these substances, which prevents their break down and increases their levels in the blood. Drugs given to treat depression have a long half-life, and it may take several weeks to see a benefit from these drugs. In addition, many adult patients find the side effects of these drugs, particularly weight gain and sexual dysfunction, to be unacceptable, so noncompliance may be a concern in the older adolescent. Other reactions of concern include extrapyramidal reactions (tremors, dystonic movements of the face and neck) and serotonin syndrome, including hypertension (Burns, Brady, Dunn & Starr, 2000; Walsh & McDougle, 2000; Wynne, Woo & Millard, 2002).

Selective Serotonin Reuptake Inhibitors (SSRI)

These are the safest of the antidepressant drugs available. They do not block other receptor sites as do the TCAs but are cytochrome p-450 enzyme inhibitors. These drugs are safe for use in the pediatric population but are not indicated for use in phobic disorders or post-traumatic stress; they should not be abruptly discontinued.

Indications: Depression, obsessive-compulsive disorder (OCD).

Actions: Inhibit serotonin reuptake and increase the serum concentration.

Drugs in class: fluoxetine (Prozac®)
paroxetine (Paxil®) - also used in panic disorder and social phobias
sertraline (Zoloft®)
citalopram (Celexa™)

Fluoxetine (Prozac)

Pregnancy risk category: B

Contraindications: Hypersensitivity to the drug or components, patients on MAOIs.

Side Effects

Cardiovascular: Not significant.

Respiratory: Not significant.

GI-GU: Nausea, diarrhea, dry mouth, constipation, weight loss, anorexia.

Dermatological: Rash, pruritus.

Hematological: Hypoglycemia, hyponatremia, especially in volume depleted patients.

Neurological: Headache, nervousness, insomnia, drowsiness, dizziness, extrapyramidal reactions.

Miscellaneous: Visual disturbances, tremor, allergies, **anaphylactic reaction**.

Food interactions: Tryptophan supplements may increase side effects, serotonin syndrome.

Drug interactions: MAOIs increase neurological side effects, may increase effects of TCAs, displaces protein-bound drugs.

Tricyclic Antidepressants (TCAs)

These are not first-line drugs for use in pediatric depression due to their side effects and the availability of safer alternative medications. These drugs also have a long half-life, requiring up to four weeks for effects to be achieved.

Indications: Depression, sedative side effects helpful in insomnia or agitation, also used in the treatment of pain.

Actions: Inhibit reuptake of norepinephrine and serotonin, block histamine and alpha 1 receptor sites.

Drugs in class: Amitryptyline (Elavil®) - used for depression, also in the treatment of migraine headaches.
imipramine (Tofranil) - also used in the treatment of nocturnal enuresis
desipramine (Noripramine®) - also used in the treatment of ADHD
doxapin (Adapin®).

Amitryptyline - Elavil

Pregnancy risk category: D

Contraindications: Sensitivity to the drug, components, or other TCAs, use of MAOIs.

Side Effects (most marked reactions are anticholinergic and sedation)

Cardiovascular: Postural hypotension, **arrhythmias, tachycardia, sudden death.**

Respiratory: Not significant.

GI-GU: Dry mouth, constipation, GE reflux, weight gain, increased appetite, urinary retention.

Dermatological: Photosensitivity.

Hematological: Elevated liver enzymes, cholestatic jaundice, **agranulocytosis, leukopenia**, eosinophilia.

Neurological: Tremor, weakness, sedation, fatigue, anxiety, confusion, **seizures**, extrapyramidal reactions.

Miscellaneous: Syndrome of inappropriate antidiuretic hormone (SIADH), blurred vision.

Food interactions: May need riboflavin supplement.

Drug interactions: Increases the effects of CNS depressants, anticholinergics and adrenergics; with MAOIs fever, tachycardia, hypertension, and death have been reported; cimetidine, fluoxetine, and methylphenidate decrease the metabolism, and phenobarbital increases the metabolism of these drugs; oral contraceptives increase drug levels.

Monoamine Oxidase Inhibitors (MAOIs)

These drugs are not first-line drugs and are rarely used in pediatric patients due to their serious side effects and the availability of safer alternatives. These drugs have a long half-life, requiring up to four weeks for effects to be achieved. Hypertensive crisis may be precipitated when these drugs are combined with tyramine-containing foods such as wine and cheese.

Actions: Inhibit breakdown of neurotransmitters.

Drugs in class: phenylzine (Nardil)
tranylcypromine (Parnate)

Miscellaneous and Newer Antidepressants

Bupropion (Wellbutrin®) - second generation antidepressant, also used for smoking cessation and ADHD, may cause arrhythmias.

Trazodone (Desyrel®) - second generation antidepressant, used in mild depression, may cause orthostatic hypotension and arrhythmias.

Nefazodone (Serzone®) - atypical antidepressant, may cause drowsiness and gastrointestinal distress.

Venlafaxine (Effexor®) - SSRI-type antidepressant, used in severe depression, may cause gastrointestinal distress.

Mirtazapine (Remeron®) - atypical antidepressant, may cause gastrointestinal distress and agranulocytosis.

Antipsychotics

These drugs are used in pediatrics mainly to treat nausea and vomiting, particularly related to chemotherapy, and exert their action by blocking dopamine receptors. Drugs in class include

- chlorpromazine (Thorazine®);
- droperidol (Inapsine®);
- haloperidol (Haldol®) - also used to treat Tourette syndrome and severe behavioral problems;
- prochlorperazine (Compazine®); and
- thioridazine (Mellaril®) - used to treat severe behavior problems.

Chlorpromazine (Thorazine)

Pregnancy risk category: C

Contraindications: Sensitivity to the drug or other phenothiazines; bone marrow suppression, liver or renal disease. May cause significant hypotension if given intravenously, injectable form contains sulfites that may cause an allergic reaction.

Side Effects

Cardiovascular: Orthostatic hypotension, arrhythmias.

Respiratory: Not significant.

GI-GU: Dry mouth, constipation, GI upset, weight gain, urinary retention, impotence.

Dermatological: Pruritus, hyperpigmentation, rash, photosensitivity.

Hematological: **Agranulocytosis, thrombocytopenia, hemolytic anemia**, eosinophilia, cholestatic jaundice.

Neurological: Sedation, restlessness, anxiety, extrapyramidal reactions, tardive dyskinesia, **seizures**, altered temperature regulation.

Miscellaneous: Blurred vision, amenorrhea, galactorrhea, gynecomastia, thrombophlebitis, **anaphylactic reactions.**

Food interactions: Interferes with riboflavin metabolism, decreases B-12 absorption.

Drug interactions: Additive effects with other CNS depressants; *hypo*tension with co-administration of epinephrine; absorption may be decreased with use of antacids; may alter serum phenytoin levels.

Antianxiolytics

Used to treat general anxiety, panic disorder, obsessive-compulsive disorder, post-traumatic stress syndrome, status epilepticus, and preoperative sedation. The major classification of drugs used is the benzodiazepines, which act by depressing the CNS including the limbic and reticular formation systems. These drugs modulate gamma aminobutyric acid (GABA), a potent inhibitory neurotransmitter. Major concerns with this classification of drugs include tolerance, abuse, and dependence. Drugs in class include

- alprazolam (Xanax®);
- chlordiazepoxide (Librium®);
- clonazepam (Klonopin®);
- diazepam (Valium®);
- lorazepam (Ativan®); and
- oxazepam (Serax®).

Lorazepam (Ativan)

Pregnancy risk category: D

Contraindications: Sensitivity to the drug or others in class, pre-existing coma or CNS depression, severe hypotension or pain.

Side Effects

Cardiovascular: **Bradycardia, circulatory collapse,** hyper- or hypotension.

Respiratory: **Respiratory depression, apnea.**

GI-GU: Constipation, dry mouth, nausea, vomiting, urinary incontinence or retention.

Dermatological: Not significant.

Hematological: Not significant.

Neurological: CNS depression, confusion, dizziness, hallucinations, myoclonic jerking in infants.

Miscellaneous: Pain at injection site, diplopia, nystagmus, physical or psychological dependence.

Food interactions: Not significant.

Drug interactions: Potentiates effects of other CNS depressants.

ATTENTION DEFICIT HYPERACTIVITY DISORDER (ADHD)

The most common neurobehavioral disorder of childhood is attention deficit hyperactivity disorder (ADHD), a complex condition characterized by three categories of symptoms: inattention, hyperactivity, and/or impulsiveness. Significant learning or behavioral problems may co-exist with ADHD, including depression, obsessive-compulsive or conduct disorder. The diagnosis of this disorder is complex and requires that symptoms be present prior to the age of seven years and for at least six months, in more than one setting such as home and school or day care, be disruptive to the child's functioning, and not be attributable to an organic cause. In younger children, the hallmark finding is impulsivity, while older children tend to manifest distractibility. ADHD may persist to adulthood, although older children and adults are able to compensate for their symptoms.

The underlying pathophysiology is an imbalance of the neurotransmitters dopamine and serotonin. Dopamine regulates activity and locomotion, and serotonin regulates mood and inhibits aggressive and impulsive behavior. In ADHD, dopamine production is increased. It is felt that stimulants work by releasing serotonin, which has an inhibitory effect on dopamine. Recent research has identified an agent that is a marker for dopamine transporters and can be documented on brain scans. This substance will greatly facilitate the diagnosis of illnesses marked by dopamine imbalance such as ADHD and Parkinson's disease.

The treatment of ADHD is three-pronged—behavioral management, maximization of school performance and achievement, and pharmacological management. Drugs used to treat ADHD include stimulants and TCAs. When using stimulants, growth parameters should be checked routinely. Low doses of stimulants are used in the inattention form of ADHD, while higher doses may be used in the hyperactive or combination types of ADHD.

Frequently ADHD co-exists with other disorders such as obsessive-compulsive disorder, depression or anxiety. In these entities antidepressant medications may be added. Many adjunctive drugs used to treat ADHD are not FDA approved for that purpose but are accepted as useful (DiTrapano, 2001; Glod, 2001).

Stimulants

Actions: Block reuptake of dopamine.

Drugs in class: methylphenidate (Ritalin®) - should not be taken in the evening due to insomnia

extended release methylphenidate (Concerta®) - has the benefit of once a day dosing
dextroamphetamine (Dexedrine®, Dexastat®) - acidic foods delay absorption
amphetamine salts (Adderal®) - long acting amphetamine
pemoline (Cylert®) - used rarely due to liver damage

Methylphenidate - Ritalin

Pregnancy risk category: C

Contraindications: Sensitivity to the drug or components, glaucoma, tics, marked agitation or anxiety.

Side Effects

Cardiovascular: Tachycardia, hypertension or hypotension, arrhythmias.

Respiratory: Not significant.

GI-GU: Anorexia, nausea, abdominal pain, weight loss.

Dermatological: Rash.

Hematological: Thrombocytopenia.

Neurological: Nervousness, insomnia, dizziness, fever, headache, hyperactivity.

Miscellaneous: Hypersensitivity reaction, tolerance.

Food interactions: Food increases absorption.

Drug interactions: Increases levels of TCAs, phenobarbital, and phenytoin, may be potentiated by MAOIs.

Antidepressants

(*See* Psychiatric Section for a discussion of these medications)

Antidepressants are used to treat co-existing conduct behavioral problems and include

- tricyclics: Imipramine, desipramine, nortryptyline.
- SSRIs: Fluoxetine, paroxetine, sertraline.
- Miscellaneous antidepressants: Wellbutrin, MAOIs, Risperdal®.

Antihypertensives

(*See* Cardiac Section for a discussion of these medications)

Anti-hypertensives are used mainly to decrease jitteriness that may accompany ADHD, and include: clonidine (Catapres), nadolol (Corguard®), propranolol (Inderal), guanfacine (Tenex®).

SEIZURE MEDICATIONS

In pediatric patients there are three classifications of seizures:

Partial - simple - localized to one hemisphere and demonstrates no change in level of consciousness.

Partial - complex - begins in one hemisphere, may spread, and results in change in level of consciousness.

Generalized - affect both hemispheres and results in change in level of consciousness. These are further broken down into:

a. Absence - in which there is staring, and the patient is unaware of their surroundings.
b. Myoclonic - stiffening of extremities.
c. Clonic - jerking of extremities.
d. Tonic - muscle spasm.
e. Tonic clonic - muscle spasms followed by jerking of extremities.

The goals of seizure therapy are to identify and correct the underlying cause if possible, reduce the alterations in cerebral blood flow, prevent depletion of energy substrates, and minimize long term sequelae of seizure activity in the brain. Drugs used to treat seizures are chosen based on classification of seizure activity.

Febrile seizures occur predominantly in children between the ages of 3 months and five years and may be classified as either simple or complex.

Simple seizures are generalized, brief in duration, and tonic-clonic in nature. Because the rate of rise of the fever is a contributing factor in the development of febrile seizures, pharmacological treatment consists of administration of antipyretic medications at the onset of the febrile episode. Complex febrile seizures are longer in duration, may occur in multiple episodes, and are focal in nature. These seizures may be caused by an underlying neurological abnormality and when that is the case may be associated with later development of epilepsy and developmental delays. Treatment of these seizures is controversial, and prophylaxis with antiseizure medication is not routinely recommended.

Diazepam has been most commonly used; phenobarbital requires a therapeutic blood level, so it is not appropriate for acute episodes (Kopec, 2001).

Carbamazepine (Tegretol®)

Pregnancy risk category: D

Action: Decreases synaptic transmission by limiting sodium ion influx.

Indication: Partial seizures.

Contraindications: Patients with a history of bone marrow suppression, sensitivity to the drug or components, TCA antidepressants, patients taking MAOIs.

Note - Generic carbamazepine and Tegretol are not equivalent, levels should be followed when switching between products; monitoring during therapy should include liver, CBC studies, and drug levels.

Side Effects

  Cardiovascular: Edema, CHF, arrhythmias, heart block.

  Respiratory: Not significant.

  GI-GU: Nausea, vomiting, diarrhea, abdominal pain, urinary retention, pancreatitis.

  Dermatological: Rash, **Stevens-Johnson syndrome.**

  Hematological: **Potentially fatal blood cell abnormalities** - early signs include; fever, sore throat, mouth ulcers, bruising, petechial rashes.

  Neurological: Sedation, dizziness, drowsiness, fatigue, confusion.

  Miscellaneous: Hepatitis, nystagmus, blurred vision.

Food interactions: Should be given with food to decrease GI upset.

Drug interactions: Carbamazepine interacts with many drugs, some of these interactions include: Macrolide antibiotics, antifungals, calcium channel blockers, cimetidine inhibit metabolism of the drug; metabolism is increased in use with oral contraceptives, phenytoin, theophylline, benzodiazepines, and steroids.

Phenobarbital

Pregnancy risk category: D

Action: Depresses CNS activity by enhancing gamma amino butyric acid (GABA) activity.

Indication: Generalized seizures.

Contraindications: Sensitivity to the drug or components, pre-existing CNS depression, severe pain or respiratory depression.

Side Effects

  Cardiovascular: **Hypotension, circulatory collapse.**

  Respiratory: **Respiratory depression, apnea.**

  GI-GU: Not significant.

  Dermatological: Rash, exfoliative dermatitis.

  Hematological: Megaloblastic anemia.

  Neurological: Drowsiness, paradoxical excitement, cognitive impairment, short term memory deficits, ataxia.

  Miscellaneous: Hepatitis, dependence.

Food interactions: Pyridoxine may decrease effects, increases metabolism of vitamins D and K, may need to supplement vitamins D, K, B12, folate, and calcium

Drug interactions: Phenobarbital has many drug interactions, among them: Phenobarbital decreases the effects of lamotrigine, oral contraceptives, griseofulvin, doxycycline, beta blockers, theophylline, steroids, tricyclic antidepressants (TCAs). Serum levels of phenobarbital may be increased by valproic acid, methylphenidate, chloramophenicol. CNS and respiratory depression are increased with the use of phenobarbital and benzodiazepines.

Valproic Acid, Valproate (Depakote®)

Pregnancy risk category: D

Action: Enhances GABA activity.

Indication: Absence seizures.

Contraindications: Sensitivity to the drug or components.

Side Effects

Cardiovascular: Not significant.

Respiratory: Not significant.

GI-GU: Nausea, vomiting, diarrhea, constipation, pancreatitis, weight gain.

Dermatological: Alopecia, erythema multiforme.

Hematological: Thrombocytopenia, elevated liver enzymes, hyperammonemia, carnitine deficiency, impaired fatty acid metabolism.

Neurological: Drowsiness, irritability, confusion, restlessness, hyperactivity, headache.

Miscellaneous: **Liver failure (may be fatal),** pain at injection site, tremor, blurred vision.

Food interactions: May require carnitine supplement, food decreases the rate of absorption.

Drug interactions: Displaces phenytoin and diazepam, may be displaced by aspirin, increases phenobarbital levels, antacids increase absorption.

Phenytoin (Dilantin)

Pregnancy risk category: D

Action: Stabilizes neuronal membranes, decreases influx of sodium ions.

Indication: Tonic clonic and partial seizures.

Contraindications: Hypersensitivity to the drug or components, heart block or bradycardia.

Side Effects

Cardiovascular: **Hypotension, bradycardia, arrhythmias, cardiovascular collapse.**

Respiratory: Not significant.

GI-GU: Nausea, vomiting, gum hyperplasia and sensitivity.

Dermatological: Hirsutism, coarseness of facial features, **Stevens-Johnson syndrome,** rash.

Hematological: Blood dyscrasias, pseudolymphoma, **lymphoma**, folic acid depletion, hyperglycemia.

Neurological: Dose related - dizziness, slurred speech, lethargy, **coma**, ataxia, dyskinesias, fever, mood changes.

Miscellaneous: Lymphadenopathy, SLE like syndrome, hepatitis.

Food interactions: May require supplements of vitamins D, K, B-12, and folate, as well as calcium, but do not give calcium and magnesium with dose.

Drug interactions: Phenytoin has many drug interactions:

Drugs whose effectiveness is *decreased*: Lamotrigine, oral contraceptives, valproic acid, steroids, theophylline, doxycycline.

Phenytoin levels may be *increased* with: Cimetidine, chloramphenicol, isoniazid, trimethoprim.

Phenytoin levels may be *decreased* with: Antineoplastics, rifampin, antacids, folic acid.

Gabapentin (Narontin®)

Pregnancy risk category: C

Action: Unknown, may exert action similar to GABA, although does not affect GABA.

Indication: Tonic-clonic, simple, complex partial seizures.

Contraindications: Sensitivity to the drug or components.

Side Effects

   Cardiovascular: Not significant.

   Respiratory: Not significant.

   GI-GU: Nausea, vomiting, weight gain, constipation, impotence.

   Dermatological: Rash.

   Hematological: Leukopenia.

   Neurological: Somnolence, dizziness, fatigue, depression, nervousness, behavioral changes such as hyperactivity, aggression, oppositional and conduct disorders.

   Miscellaneous: Diplopia, nystagmus, back pain, tremor, arthralgia.

Food interactions: Not significant.

Drug interactions: Antacids decrease absorption, cimetidine may decrease clearance.

OPHTHALMOLOGIC MEDICATIONS

Mydriatics are medications used to dilate pupils for ophthalmologic examinations in the pediatric patient.

Mydriatics

Action: Dilate pupil to facilitate examination of the retinal fundus.

Side effects: Bradycardia, **apnea** or hypertension (medication or procedure induced).

Drugs in class: cyclopentolate 0.5% (Cyclogel®)
cyclomyadril phenylephrine 1%
neosynephrine 0.2%
mydriacil 0.5%

EXAM QUESTIONS

CHAPTER 5
Questions 40–48

40. The gateway theory of pain perception describes

    a. the conduction of sharp pain sensation.

    b. the maturity of pain perception once nerves are myelinized.

    c. intensification of pain perception with agitation or anticipation.

    d. pain perception is altered by nonpharmacological pain relief methods.

41. Pain responses in the young child include

    a. deep sleep.

    b. tachycardia.

    c. habituation.

    d. acidosis.

42. A common pain medication rarely given to children is

    a. Tylenol.

    b. morphine.

    c. ibuprofen.

    d. aspirin.

43. The pharmacodynamics of antidepressant medication includes

    a. facilitation of reuptake of neurotransmitters.

    b. inhibition of the P-450 enzyme system.

    c. blockade of reuptake of neurotransmitters.

    d. facilitation of conversion of tyramine to epinephrine.

44. An antihypertensive medication also used in the treatment of ADHD to decrease jitteriness is

    a. prazosin (Minipress).

    b. captopril (Capoten).

    c. clonidine (Catapres).

    d. atenolol (Tenormin).

45. A medication which may be used in a child with ADHD and co-existing conduct disorder is

    a. desipramine (Noripramine).

    b. clonidine (Catapres).

    c. pemoline (Cylert).

    d. lorazepam (Ativan).

46. A concern with the use of antidepressants in children is

    a. children metabolize these medications differently than adults.

    b. side effects of these medications are insignificant.

    c. effects of these medications may take several weeks to be noted.

    d. children do not tolerate these medications.

47. One of the goals in treatment of seizures is

    a. regulation of cerebral blood flow.
    b. facilitation of state control.
    c. prevention of drug dependence.
    d. prevention of intraventricular hemorrhage.

48. A side effect of mydriatics used for ophthalmologic examinations is

    a. prolonged mydriasis.
    b. prolonged miosis.
    c. bradycardia.
    d. neovascularization.

CHAPTER 6

DERMATOLOGICAL MEDICATIONS

CHAPTER OBJECTIVE

After completing this chapter, the reader will be able to specify the classifications of dermatological medications and indicate the applicable nursing implications for the administration of these drugs.

LEARNING OBJECTIVES

At the completion of the chapter, the reader will be able to

1. recognize which dermatological medications are commonly used in the pediatric population.
2. specify common conditions in the pediatric population that may benefit from the administration of these medications.
3. recognize common side effects of the use of these medications.

SKIN LESIONS

Dermatological conditions are among the most difficult to diagnose in the pediatric population. The skin is divided into three layers—the uppermost layer, epidermis; the middle or dermis layer, and the innermost hypodermis. Rashes and skin abnormalities may be described using the following terminology:

- *Macule* - a flat, nonpalpable, circumscribed area of discoloration. Mongolian spots or freckles are an example of macules.
- *Plaque* - a flat, often rough area such as is found in eczema or psoriasis.
- *Vesicle* - a small fluid-filled sac, the rash of poison ivy is an example.
- *Papule* - a solid, raised mass, usually less than 0.5 cm.
- *Nodule* - a papule that is larger than 0.5 cm.
- *Pustule* - a vesicle that contains purulent material.
- *Wheal* - an erythematous raised area, such as might be seen in an allergic reaction.
- *Bulla* - a larger fluid-filled vesicle.

This discussion will focus on the more common skin conditions in the pediatric population: atopic dermatitis (eczema), impetigo, acne, fungal infections (the tineas), and infestations of lice, pinworms, and scabies.

Atopic dermatitis is also known as eczema and is commonly seen in infants and children but may persist to adulthood. The condition is genetically determined and associated with allergies. In infants the characteristic papulo-vesicular rash is found on the cheeks, forehead, scalp, and trunk, as well as *extensor* surfaces of the extremities. These lesions often are accompanied by oozing and crusting. In older children the condition is characterized by scaly, dry, pruritic skin on the trunk, ears, neck and *flexor* surfaces of the extremities. In adolescents the condition may develop a leathery, scaly appearance. Treatment includes drying agents for moist lesions and emollients for dry lesions. Steroids may be used topically for localized lesions and orally for more widespread involvement. Antihistamines may be used to treat the pruritis that accompanies the disorder (Sidbury & Hanifin, 2000). (See Respiratory Medications section for a discussion of these medications.)

Impetigo is one of the most contagious skin conditions in infants and children. Predisposing factors to the condition include crowded living spaces, poor personal hygiene, presence of insect bites, pre-existing atopic dermatitis, and cutaneous injury. The condition is characterized by the presence of discrete papules progressing to pustules that, when they rupture produce a honey colored crust, the hallmark of the condition. The causative infectious agent is *staphylococcus aureus*. The treatment is topical mupirocin (Bactroban®) for localized infections and penicillin for extensive involvement.

Mupirocin (Bactroban)

Pregnancy risk category: B

Contraindications: Sensitivity to the drug or components, or to polyethylene glycol.

Side Effects

Cardiovascular: Not significant.

Respiratory: Not significant.

GI-GU: Not significant.

Dermatological: Rash, urticaria, erythema, dry skin, burning, stinging, local edema.

Hematological: Not significant.

Neurological: Not significant.

Miscellaneous: Potentially toxic amounts of polyethylene glycol may be absorbed in patients with extensive skin involvement.

Food interactions: Not significant.

Drug interactions: Lithium and potassium iodide may potentiate effects, enhances effects of warfarin.

Fungal infections include the tineas: *tinea capitis,* a fungal infection of the scalp, characterized by scaly plaques, and erythematous areas with broken hairs at the level of the scalp; *tinea corporis,* characterized by mild itching and scaly raised areas with pink borders; *tinea cruris,* or tinea of the groin and upper thighs ("jock itch") characterized by red raised areas with itching and pain or tenderness in the groin area; *tinea pedis,* (or "athlete's foot"), characterized by reddened scaly, blistered itchy areas between the toes. These conditions are treated with oral antifungals such as griseofulvin (Capitis®) or a topical antifungal such as clotrimazole.

Clotrimazole - Lotrimin®

Pregnancy risk category: B (topical), C (troches)

Contraindications: Sensitivity to the drug or components.

Side Effects (side effects are mostly seen with use of vaginal applications for fungal infections)

Cardiovascular: Not significant.

Respiratory: Not significant.

GI-GU: Nausea, vomiting, and abdominal pain with use of troches (vaginal suppositories).

Dermatological: Erythema, pruritis, urticaria, fissures, blistering.

Hematological: Abnormal liver function studies (rare).

Neurological: Not significant.

Miscellaneous: Mild burning, irritation of vaginal area.

Food interactions: Not significant.

Drug interactions: Not significant.

Pediculosis (lice) is a highly contagious condition affecting hairy parts of the body; the causative agent is a parasitic louse. Hallmark findings include presence of nits of the lice, which appear as removable white flakes, and itching. *Scabies* is a contagious condition caused by the mite *sarcoptes scabiei*. The hallmark findings of scabies in infants are vesicles on the head, neck, palms and soles; in older children red papular lesions are found in intertriginous areas, the axillae, waist, buttocks, groin, abdomen and knees. As the mites burrow under the skin linear, curved burrows may be seen. These are often subtle and difficult to see. The presence of pustules indicates secondary bacterial infection. Pharmacological intervention for both scabies and pediculosis includes topical application of permethrin (Forfia, 2001).

Permethrin - Elimite®, Nix®

Pregnancy risk category: B

Contraindications: Sensitivity to pyrethroid, pyrethrin, or components, or sensitivity to chrysanthemums.

Side Effects

Cardiovascular: Not significant.

Respiratory: Not significant.

GI-GU: Not significant.

Dermatological: Pruritis, erythema, rash.

Hematological: Not significant.

Neurological: Numbness, tingling.

Miscellaneous: Burning, stinging, edema, pain at site of application.

Food interactions: Not significant.

Drug interactions: Not significant.

Pinworms, or *enterobiasis vermicularis,* are nematodes that infest the rectum, emerging at night to lay eggs, resulting in nocturnal itching, the hallmark of the condition. Occasionally worm-like threads may be visible in the child's underwear or in the toilet. The condition is treated with an antihelminthic agent, mebendazole (Vermox®).

Mebendazole - Vermox

Pregnancy risk category: C

Contraindications: Sensitivity to the drug or components.

Side Effects

Cardiovascular: Not significant.

Respiratory: Not significant.

GI-GU: Diarrhea, abdominal pain, nausea, vomiting, hematuria.

Dermatological: Rash, pruritis, alopecia.

Hematological: Neutropenia, anemia, leukopenia, transient abnormalities in liver studies.

Neurological: Not significant.

Miscellaneous: Tinnitus.

Food interactions: Food increases absorption.

Drug interactions: Antiseizure medications may increase metabolism.

Acne is the most common skin condition in adolescents, affecting up to 90% of children in this age group. Contributing factors include hormonal changes, increased sebaceous gland activity, increased sebum production, and oxidization of sebum. Comedones are the classical finding; oxidized sebum gives them a dark appearance (blackheads). When *corynebacterium acnes* is present, the comedones develop a pustular appearance and become inflamed leading to cystic pitting and scarring. Nonpharmacological therapy includes diet and lifestyle changes, encouraging exercise and rest. Pharmacological treatment includes use of benzoyl peroxide washes for mild acne, topical tetracycline, erythromycin, or clindamycin for pustules and cystic acne, and retinoic acid for severe cases of acne (Mancini, 2000).

Tretinoin - Retin-A® (topical formulation)

Pregnancy risk category: C

Contraindications: Sensitivity to the drug or components, sunburn.

Side Effects: *Significant side effects are seen with oral formulation; topical formulation produces mainly dermatological side effects.

Cardiovascular: Not significant.

Respiratory: Not significant.

GI-GU: Not significant.

Dermatological: Excessive dryness, erythema, hyper- or hypopigmentation, photosensitivity, avoid contact with abraded skin and mucous membranes.

Hematological: Not significant.

Neurological: Not significant.

Miscellaneous: Stinging and blistering.

Drug interactions: Preparations containing salicylic acid, sulfur compounds, and benzoyl peroxide potentiate dermatological reactions.

Food interactions: Avoid excess intake of vitamin A.

EXAM QUESTIONS

CHAPTER 6
Questions 49–53

49. The medication of choice for mild acne is

   a. benzoyl peroxide.
   b. tretinoin.
   c. clindamycin.
   d. erythromycin.

50. The medication of choice for scabies is

   a. mupirocin.
   b. mebendazole.
   c. Cipro.
   d. permethrin.

51. The hallmark finding in impetigo is

   a. dry plaques.
   b. honey-colored crusts.
   c. vesicles and papules.
   d. erythematous pustules.

52. The drug of choice for impetigo is

   a. mebendazole.
   b. mupirocin.
   c. permethrin.
   d. tretinoin.

53. A useful drug that has significant side effects is

   a. oral mebendazole.
   b. oral tretinoin.
   c. topical permethrin.
   d. topical tretinoin.

This concludes the final examination. An answer key will be sent with your certificate so that you can determine which of your answers were correct and incorrect.

APPENDIX 1

SUMMARY OF DRUG INTERACTIONS

- **Dose-related reaction** - related to overdose or other factors that would result in elevated drug levels, such as the P-450 enzyme system or decreased protein binding.
- **Idiosyncratic reaction** - individualized, unpredictable reaction.
- **Side effect reaction** - predictable based on pharmacology of the drug.
- **Allergic reaction** - individual sensitivity to a drug, ranging from GI symptoms to anaphylaxis.
- **Drug-drug reaction** - interactions seen when drugs affect the metabolism of or potentiate the effects of other drugs.

APPENDIX 2

SUMMARY OF FACTORS AFFECTING DRUG THERAPY IN THE VERY YOUNG CHILD

Factors That Affect Absorption

    decreased muscle mass

    decreased peripheral perfusion

    increased skin water content

    skin fragility

    slower GI transit time

    enterohepatic circulation

    decreased receptor sites

    lower pH of plasma

    higher pH of GI tract

Factors That Affect Distribution

    variable V_d

    decreased fat tissue

    higher body water content

Factors That Affect Elimination

    immature enzyme systems

    immature renal function

Factors That Affect Administration Routes

    decreased plasma proteins

    decreased affinity for protein binding

    competition for binding sites

APPENDIX 3

CALCULATING DOSAGES

Some important tips:

a. Keep units consistent; if drug is prescribed in milligrams, calculate those first, then calculate the volume.
b. Three terms to remember:

   concentration - expressed in milligrams or millequivalents per milliliter, usually

   dose - expressed in milligrams or millequivalents per kilogram, usually

   volume - expressed in milliliters

EXAMPLE 1

Drug	Concentration	Dose	Volume
sodium bicarbonate	0.5 meq/ml	2 meq/kg	4 ml/kg

1. *Question:* how many mls would you draw up for a 2 meq dose? Set up the equation this way: What you *have* (the concentration) on one side, what you *need* (the dose) on the other.

$$\frac{0.5 \text{ meq}}{1 \text{ ml}} \quad : \quad \frac{2 \text{ meq}}{X}$$

2. Then cross multiply so that: $0.5 X = 2$
3. Divide both sides by 0.5 and solve for X: $X = \frac{2}{0.5}$

$$X = 4 \text{ ml}$$

An easier way to think about this one is: If 0.5 meq are in one ml, how many mls does it take to give 1 meq? The answer is 2 mls. Thus, if the dose is 2 meq, the volume is 4 mls.

EXAMPLE 2

Drug	Concentration	Dose	Volume
Narcan	0.4 mg/ml	0.1 mg/kg	0.25 cc/kg

1. *Question:* how much Narcan would you draw up for a 0.1 mg dose? Again, set up the concentration on one side and the dose needed on the other side:

$$\frac{0.4 \text{ mg}}{1 \text{ ml}} \quad : \quad \frac{0.1 \text{ mg}}{X}$$

Cross multiply and solve for X:

$$0.4 X = 0.1$$
$$X = \frac{0.1}{0.4}$$
$$x = 0.25 \text{ cc}$$

APPENDIX 4

RESUSCITATION MEDICATIONS

Medication	Concentration	Dose	Volume
1. Narcan	0.4 mg/ml	0.1 mg/kg	0.25 ml/kg

Indication: Respiratory depression and maternal narcotic four hours before delivery.

Use cautiously in infants whose history is unknown, may cause withdrawal seizures.

Medication	Concentration	Dose	Volume
2. Epinephrine	1:10000	0.01 mg/kg	0.1–0.3 ml/kg
	1:1000		

Indication: heart rate less than sixty with good ventilations.

1:10000 concentration given IV, 1:1000 concentration may be given through the endotracheal tube.

Medication	Concentration	Dose	Volume
3. Sodium Bicarbonate	4.2% for neonates (0.5 meq/ml)	2 meq/kg	4 ml/kg of 4.2%
	8.4% for pediatrics (1 meq/ml)	0.5–1 meq/kg	0.5–1 ml/kg

Indications: Documented acidosis or given without during prolonged resuscitation.

Medication	Concentration	Dose	Volume
4. Volume expanders	-	-	10 cc/kg

Include normal saline, lactated ringer's solution, whole blood and 5% albumin.

Medication	Concentration	Dose	Volume
5. Dopamine	40 mg/ml	6 X weight in kg X required dose = required IV rate	
		This will give the milligrams to add to 100 mls of D5W.	
		milligrams to add to 100 cc = 40	
		This will give volume to add to 100 ml of D5W.	

A faster calculation is to add 30 mg (0.75 ml) of dopamine to 100 ml D5W and run the IV rate at the baby's weight in Kg (i.e., 2 kg = 2 cc/h). This will give **5 mcg/kg/min.**

Medication	Concentration	Dose	Volume
6. Atropine	0.1–1 mg/ml	0.02 mg/kg	0.1–1 ml
		minimum dose 0.1 mg	

Source: Kattwinkel, J. (Ed). (2000). *Manual of Neonatal Resuscitation.* Elk Grove Village, IL: American Academy of Pediatrics.

APPENDIX 5

PREGNANCY RISK CATEGORIES

CATEGORY A - studies in women have found that the risk of harm in pregnancy is remote.

CATEGORY B - animal studies show no risk, but human studies have not been done, or human risk has not been verified with controlled studies.

CATEGORY C - animal studies have demonstrated risk or there are no studies in humans. These drugs should only be used if the risk justifies the potential harm to the fetus.

CATEGORY D - evidence of risk to the fetus but the benefit may justify the risk (i.e., life threatening situation).

CATEGORY X - clear evidence of harm, risk outweighs any benefit to the mother. These medications are contraindicated.

APPENDIX 6

INTRAOSSEOUS INFUSION

1. **Indications** - for rapid infusion in cardiopulmonary failure when standard methods of access have failed.

2. **Procedure** -
   - identify site, should be flat with good bony landmarks
   - sites include:
     — medial surface of proximal tibia 2–3 cm distal to the tuberosity
     — distal tibia 2-3 cm proximal to the malleolus
     — midline of lower third of femur 3–4 cms above the condyle
   - place a roll under the knee to position the femur or tibia
   - clean site with Betadine®
   - using intraosseous needle, insert through skin then aim slightly downward, away from the growth plate
   - when bone is reached exert downward pressure in a twisting motion
   - confirm placement by withdrawal of marrow tissue and rigid position of the needle in the bone
   - connect IV fluids and infuse

GLOSSARY

Absorption - A term that describes the movement of a drug into the circulation after administration.

Active diffusion - When molecules of drugs are carried across the cell membrane. This process requires extra energy (see *Facilitated Diffusion*).

Adrenergic response - A response generated after stimulation of receptor sites by epinephrine; the "fight or flight" response.

Afterload - Resistance from the peripheral circulation presented to the heart during and after systole.

Agonist - A drug that stimulates a response from a receptor site.

Agranulocytosis - A side effect of certain drugs in which there are no discernible levels of the granulocyte white cell form.

Alopecia - A side effect of certain drugs in which there is hair loss.

Amenorrhea - A side effect of certain drugs in which there is lack of menstruation.

Antagonist - A drug that inhibits a response from a receptor site.

Anticholinergic response - A response generated after inhibition of cholinergic receptor sites, which results in dry mouth, blurred vision, and increased heart rate.

Antigen - A foreign substance that generates an immune response. Antigens may be viruses, bacteria or other substances.

Arthralgia - A side effect of certain drugs in which there is joint pain.

Ataxia - A side effect of certain drugs in which there is altered gait.

Autonomic nervous system - The part of the nervous system that produces a "fight or flight" response after stimulation of its receptor sites by epinephrine.

Cholinergic response - A response generated after stimulation of receptor sites by acetylcholine that results in increased secretions, increased gastrointestinal motility and decreased heart rate.

Cytochrome p-450 enzyme system - An enzyme system in the liver involved in the metabolism of medications.

Dead space overdose - A term used to describe the overdose that can occur when a syringe used to administer a medication is flushed while still connected to the intravenous line. There is a small amount of medication that remains in the hub of the syringe that is inadvertently administered.

Diaphoresis - A side effect of certain drugs in which there is sweating.

Distribution - Describes movement of an administered drug from the circulation to the site of action.

Elimination - In order to be eliminated a drug must first be inactivated. Drugs are eliminated primarily through the kidneys.

Erythema multiforme - A side effect of certain drugs in which there is a characteristic erythematous rash.

Extrapyramidal side effects - Side effects seen after the administration of antidepressant medications, which include abnormal movements of the face and neck and tremors.

Facilitated diffusion - A drug molecule rides across the cell membrane aboard a carrier molecule. This process does not require extra energy (see *Active Diffusion*).

First pass elimination - A term used to describe the partial breakdown of orally administered drugs. This breakdown affects the required dose of a drug.

GERD - Gastro-esophageal reflux disease, characterized by ineffective lower esophageal tone resulting in splash back of acidic gastric contents into the lower esophagus.

Gingival hyperplasia - gum overgrowth.

Immunoglobulins - Substances produced by the immune system that provide passive immunity after exposure to an antigen. Passive immunity may only last several months and is not permanent.

Inflammation - A condition that is seen particularly in respiratory illness such as asthma and occurs after exposure to triggers such as dust mites and allergens. It creates a cascade of physiologic responses that cause narrowing and irritation of the airways and production of secretions.

Left shift - A term used to describe an increased number of immature white cell forms in the circulation. The presence of a left shift is helpful in diagnosing infection.

Leukocytosis - A side effect of certain drugs in which there is a decrease in circulating leukocytes.

Lower esophageal sphincter - The sphincter, or valve, that is found at the junction between the lower esophagus and the stomach.

MDI - A metered dose inhaler is used to administer inhaled medications, particularly in asthma.

Melena - A side effect of certain drugs in which there is blood in the stools.

Myalgia - A side effect of certain drugs in which there is muscle pain.

Nephrocalcinosis - A side effect of certain drugs in which there is build up of calcium in the kidneys.

Neutropenia - A side effect of certain drugs in which there is a decrease in circulating neutrophils.

Nystagmus - A side effect of certain drugs in which there is abnormal movement of the iris of the eye.

Parasympathetic nervous system - The part of the nervous system that produces a "rest and digest" response after stimulation of its receptor sites by acetylcholine.

Passive diffusion - A drug moves across the cell membrane from an area of greater to an area of lesser concentration.

Pharmacodynamics - A term used to describe the physiologic effect medications exert in the body.

Phase one and two reactions - Chemical reactions involved in the metabolism of medications.

Pharmacokinetics - A term used to describe the movement of drugs through the body and encompasses absorption, distribution, and elimination.

Pinocytosis - A drug molecule is transported across a cell membrane after the membrane has engulfed the molecule.

PNE - Primary nocturnal enuresis is defined as unintentional leakage of urine at night.

Pore transport - A drug molecule crosses the cell membrane through openings, or pores.

Preload - A term used to describe the volume of blood presented to the heart before systole. Preload is determined primarily by blood volume.

Protein binding - Once administered drugs become bound to protein. This bound portion is inactive, and is a factor in the required dose of a medication.

Pruritis - A side effect of certain drugs in which there is itching.

Receptor sites - Sites found on target organs to which drug molecules attach in order to exert their effect.

Resistance - A term used to describe the ability antigens such as bacteria and viruses have to protect themselves against antibiotics.

Stevens-Johnson syndrome - A severe side effect of certain drugs in which there is generalized rash.

Tardive dyskinesia - A side effect of certain drugs in which there is abnormal motor activity.

Thrombocytopenia - A side effect of certain drugs in which there is a decrease in circulating platelets.

Tinnitus - A side effect of certain drugs in which there is ringing in the ears.

Urticaria - A side effect of certain drugs in which there are hives.

Vaccines - In either live or killed formulations stimulate an immune response that may last months or years. This response may be evaluated through blood titers.

BIBLIOGRAPHY

Barton, S. (2001). *Clinical Evidence.* Minneapolis: United Health Foundation.

Blumer, J. (2001). Managing Pediatric Infections. *Contemporary Pediatrics* (supplement).

Brosnan, C., Upchurch, S. & Schreiver, B. (2001). Type 2 diabetes in children and adolescents: An emerging disease. *Pediatric Health Care, 15,* 187.

Burns, C., Brady, M., Dunn, A. & Starr, N. (2000). *Pediatric Primary Care: Handbook for Nurse Practitioners* (2nd ed.). Philadelphia: W.B. Saunders.

DiTrapano, C. (2001). Are all drugs created equal? *Advance for Nurses, 1,* 22.

Flick, G. (1998). *ADD/ADHD Behavior change resource kit.* West Nyack, NJ: Center for Applied Research in Education.

Forfia, M. (2001). Lice control, the best line of defense. *Advance for Nurses, 3,* 36.

Glod, C. (2001). Attention Deficit Hyperactivity Disorder. *Advance for Nurse Practitioners, 9,* 52.

Gunn, V. & Nechyba, C. (2002). *The Harriet Lane Handbook* (16th ed.). St Louis: Mosby.

Harvey, R. & Champe, P. (1997). *Lippincott's Illustrated Reviews: Pharmacology* (2nd ed.). Philadelphia: Lippincott.

Heubi, J. (1999). Acetaminophen: The other side of the story. *Contemporary Pediatrics, 16,* 61.

Hogg, R., Landa, H., Kaplan, G., Schulman, S. & Packer, M. (2000). Nocturnal enuresis: Evaluation, education, treatment. *Contemporary Pediatrics* (supplement).

Jellin, J. (Ed). (2001). *Prescriber's Letter.* Stockton, CA: Therapeutic Research Center.

Kattwinkel, J. (Ed.). (2000). *Manual of Neonatal Resuscitation.* Elk Grove Village, IL: American Academy of Pediatrics.

Kopec, J. (2001). New anticonvulsants in pediatrics. *Journal of Pediatric Health Care, 15,* 81.

Lieberman, J. (2001). Varicella vaccine: What have we learned? *Contemporary Pediatrics, 18,* 50.

Lynn, A., Ulma, G. & Spieker, M. (1999). Pain control for very young infants: An update. *Contemporary Pediatrics, 16,* 39.

Mancini, A. (2000). Acne vulgaris: A treatment update. *Contemporary Pediatrics, 17,* 122.

McAdams, C., Heller, C. & Calandra, L. (2000). Current issues in otitis media treatment. *Advance for Nurse Practitioners, 9,* 34.

Osterhoudt, K. (2000). The toxic toddler: Drugs that can kill in one dose. *Contemporary Pediatrics, 17,* 73.

Pinhas-Hamiel, O. & Zeitler, P. (2001). Type 2 diabetes, not just for grownups anymore. *Contemporary Pediatrics, 18,* 102.

Pickering, L. (Ed). (2000). *2000 Red Book: Report of the Committee on Infectious Disease* (25th edition). Elk Grove Village, IL: American Academy of Pediatrics.

Shields, B. (2001). Prevnar: Disease prevention in infants and children. *Pediatric Health Care, 15,* 203.

Sidbury, R. & Hanifin, T. (2000). When atopic dermatitis is hard to control. *Contemporary Pediatrics, 17,* 39.

Skidmore-Roth (consultant). (2003). *Mosby's Nursing Drug Reference.* St Louis: Mosby.

Starr, C. (2000). Essentials of pediatric dosing. *Patient Care for the Nurse Practitioner, 3,* 48.

Steinbach, S. (2000). Four controversies in pediatric asthma care. *Contemporary Pediatrics, 17,* 150.

Takemoto, C., Hodding, J. & Kraus, D. (2001–2002). *Pediatric Dosage Handbook* (6th ed.). Cleveland: Lexi-Comp.

Turcios, N. (2001). What you need to know about pediatric asthma pharmacology. *Contemporary Pediatrics, 18,* 81.

Waldrop, J. (2001). A New Weapon against Pneumococcal disease. *Advance for Nurse Practitioners, 9,* 34.

Walsh, K. & McDougle, C. (2000). When SSRIs make sense. *Contemporary Pediatrics, 17,* 83.

Wilde, T. (2001). Antibiotic resistance and the problem of antibiotic overuse. *Pediatric Emergency Medicine Reports, 6,* 45.

Wynne, A., Woo, T. & Millard, M. (2002). *Pharmacotherapeutics for nurse practitioner prescribers.* Philadelphia: F.A. Davis.

Young, F. (2000). New Developments in Antibiotics. *Patient Care for the Nurse Practitioner, 3,* 25.

Young, T. & Magnum, O. (2002). *Neofax* (15th ed). Raleigh, NC: Acorn Publishing.

INDEX

A

absorption, 2-3
ACE (angiotensin converting enzyme) inhibitors, 13
acetaminophen (Tylenol), 48-49
acetazolamide (Diamox), 25
active diffusion, 2
ADHD (attention deficit hyperactivity disorder)
    antidepressants for, 55
    anti-hypertensives for, 55
    overview of, 54
    stimulants for, 54-55
Aerobid, 15
Afrin, 17-18
agonists
    cholinergic, 1-2
    defining, 1
    long-acting beta 2, 15
    pain management, 49
    short-acting beta 2, 14-15
albuterol (Proventil, Ventolin), 14-15
Aldactone, 24-25
aldosterone, 23
allergy drugs
    antihistamines, 18
    antitussives, 18-20
    decongestants, 17-18
Alpha 2 sites, 2
alpha glucosidase inhibitors, 30
Alpha 1 sites, 2
aminophylline food/drug interactions, 19-20
amitryptyfine-Elavil, 52
antacids, 27
antagonists
    defining, 1
    H2, 27-28
    inhibitors of folate reduction/folate, 41-42
    pain management, 49
antianxiolytics, 53-54
anti-arrhythmics
    class 1-sodium channel blockers, 10
    class 2-beta blockers, 10-11
    class 3-potassium channel blockers, 11
    class 4-calcium channel blockers, 11
    miscellaneous, 11-12

    overview of, 9-10
antibiotic resistance, 36-37
antibiotics
    basis of selecting, 36
    folate antagonists/inhibitors of folate reduction, 41-42
    immune response and, 35-37
    oxazolidinones classification of, 37
    that inhibit cell wall synthesis, 42-43
    that inhibit nucleic acid function, 43-44
    that inhibit protein synthesis, 43
anticholinergics, 16-17
antidepressants, 52-53
antidiuretic hormone, 23, 26
antihistamines, 18
anti-hypertensives
    for ADHD, 55
    angiotensin converting enzyme (ACE) inhibitors, 13
    central-acting ANS agents, 12
    peripheral-acting CNS agents, 13
antipsychotics, 53
antithyroid drugs, 31-32
antitussives
    guaifenesin, 18
    methylxanthines, 18-19
    theophylline/aminophylline food/drug interactions, 19-20
arrhythmias
    anti-arrhythmics used to treat, 9-12
    origins of, 9
atenolol (Tenormin), 10
Ativan, 53-54
atrial fibrillation, 9
atrial flutter, 9
Atrovent, 2, 16-17
attenuated (or weakened) vaccine, 37
autonomic central nervous system
    defining, 1
    four types of receptor sites in, 2
azithromycin (Zithromax), 43
Azmacort, 15

B

Bactrim, 41-42

B cells, 35
beclomethasone (Vanceril), 15
Beta 1 sites, 2
beta 2 agonists
    long-acting, 15
    short-acting, 14-15
Beta 2 sites, 2
beta blockers, 10-11
biguanides, 30
Bretylium (Bretylol), 11
broad spectrum drugs, 36
budesonide (Pulmicort, Pulmicort Respules), 16

C
calcium channel blockers, 11
captopril (Capoten), 13
carbamazepine (Tegretol), 56
carbonic anhydrase inhibitors, 25
cardio-respiratory drugs
    allergy treatment and, 17-20
    anti-arrhythmics, 9-12
    anti-hypertensives, 12-13
    reactive airway disease and, 13-17
Catapres, 12
CDC website, 37
ceftriaxone (Rocephin), 42-43
cell-mediated immunity (or T cell), 35
central-acting ANS agents, 13-14
chlorpromazine (Thorazine), 53
cholinergic agonists, 1-2
ciprofloxacin (Cipro), 44
clonidine (Catapres), 12
clotrimazole-Lotrimin, 62-63
Cotrim, 41-42
cromolyn (Nasalcrom, Intal), 16

D
decongestants, 17-18
Depakote, 57
depression
    pathophysiology of, 51
    psychiatric drugs for, 51-52
dermatological medications
    clotrimazole-lotrimin, 62-63
    mebendazole-vermox, 63
    mupirocin (Bactroban), 62
    permethrin-elimite, Nix, 63
    skin lesions and, 61-62
    tretinoin-Retin-A, 63-64
desmopressin (DDAVP), 26
diabetes, 29-30
diabetic medications
    alpha glucosidase inhibitors, 30
    biguanides, 30
    insulin, 30-31
Diamox, 25
digoxin (Lanoxin), 11
Dilantin, 57-58
diptheria vaccine, 39
distribution of drug, 4
diuretics
    carbonic anhydrase inhibitors, 25
    described, 23
    loop, 24
    osmotic, 25
    potassium-sparing, 24-25
    thiazide, 23-24
drugs
    administration and absorption of, 2-3
    agonists and antagonists, 1-2
    cardio-respiratory, 9-20
    dermatological, 61-64
    distribution, metabolism, elimination of, 4-5
    efficacy of, 1
    genitourinary and gastrointestinal, 23-32
    monitoring levels of, 5
    psychiatric, 51-58
DTaP (diphtheria, tetanus, and pertussis), 39

E
ECF (extracellular fluid compartment), 4
Effexor, 53
efficacy
    as antibiotic selection criteria, 36
    defining, 1
Elavil, 52
electrolyte gradients, 23
elimination of drugs, 4-5
Elimite, 63
Emla, 50
enalapril (Vasotec), 13
ergotamine, 50-51

F
facilitated diffusion, 2
fentanyl (Sublimaze), 49-50
"fight or flight" response, 1
first pass elimination, 4
Flovent, 15
fluisolide (Aerobid), 15
fluoxetine (Prozac), 51-52
fluticasone (Flovent), 15
furosemide (Lasix), 24

G
GABA (modulate gamma aminobutyric acid), 53

genitourinary/gastrointestinal medications
   diabetic medications as, 29-31
   diuretics, 23-25
   for gastroesophageal reflux (GERD), 26-29
   nutritional supplements as, 29
   for primary nocturnal enuresis, 26
   thyroid medications as, 31-32
gentamicin, 43
GERD (gastroesophageal reflux)
   antacids for, 27
   described, 26-27
   H2 antagonists for, 27-28
   prokinetics for, 28-29
   proton pump inhibitors for, 28
gestational diabetes, 29
Glucophage, 30
guaifenesin, 18

H
H2 antagonists, 27-28
headache medication, 50-51
Hepatitis B vaccine, 38, 38-39
HIB (*Haemophilus influenza* B) vaccine, 39
hydrochlorothiazide (Hydrodiuril), 23-24
Hyoscine, 2
hyperthyroidism, 31
hypothyroidism, 31

I
ibuprofen (Motrin), 48
IDDM (insulin dependent diabetes), 30
IgA immunoglobulin, 36
IgD immunoglobulin, 36
IgE immunoglobulin, 36
IgG immunoglobulin, 36
IgM immunoglobulin, 36
immune response, 35-37
immune system function, 36
immunization
   general considerations of, 37-38
   postnatal vs. postconceptual, 37
immunoglobulins, 35-36
influenza vaccine, 41
inhaled corticosteroids, 15-16
inhaled medication delivery, 3
insulin, 30-31
insulin patient teaching, 31
Intal, 16
intramuscular drug administration, 3
intravenous drug administration, 3
ipratropium (Atrovent), 2
IPV (inactivated polis virus) vaccine, 39

K
killed virus vaccine, 37

L
Lanoxin, 11
Lasix, 24
left shift, 36
LES (lower esophageal sphincter), 26, 27
leukotriene modifiers, 17
levothyroxine-Levoxyl, 31
lidocaine (Xylocaine), 10
linezolid (Zyvox), 37
lisinopril (Zestril), 13
long-acting beta 2 agonists, 15
loop diuretics, 24
lorazepam (Ativan), 53-54
Lotrimin, 62-63
lpratropium (Atrovent), 16-17
lyme (Lymerix) vaccine, 41

M
magnesium salts (Milk of Magnesia), 27
Mannitol, 25
MAOIs (monoamine oxidase inhibitors), 52-53
mast cell stabilizers, 16
MDI (metereed dose inhaler), 14
meglitinides, 30
membrane transport, 2
Meningococcal vaccine, 40-41
metabolism of drugs, 4
metformin-Glucophage, 30
methyixanthines, 18-19
methylprednisolone, 15-16
metoclopramide-Reglan, 29-30
migraine headaches, 50-51
Minipress, 13
mirtazapine (Remeron), 53
MMR (measles, mumps, rubella) vaccine, 39-40
monitoring drug levels, 5
montelukast (Singulair), 17
Motrin, 48
MRSA (methicillin-resistant *staphylococcus aureus*), 36, 37
Mycostatin, 44
mydriatics, 58

N
nalaxone (Narcan), 50
narcotics/opiates, 49-50
Narontin, 58
narrow spectrum antibiotics, 36
Nasalcrom, 16
nefazodone (Serzone), 53

neurological medications
    for headache, 50-51
        pain medications, 47-50
        psychiatric drugs, 51-53
nifedepine (Procardia), 11
Nix, 63
non-narcotic analgesics, 48-49
NSAIDS, 48
nutritional supplements, 29
nystatin (Mycostatin), 44

O

Omeprazole-Prilosec, 28
ophthalmologic medications, 58
opiates/narcotics, 49-50
orally (or enternally) drug administration, 3
osmotic diuretics, 25
oxazolidinones, 37
oxymetzoline (Afrin), 17-18

P

P-450 system, 4
PACs (premature atrial contractions), 9
pain
    key to management of, 48
    sensation and assessment of, 47
pain medications
    narcotics/opiates, 49-50
    non-narcotic analgesics, 48-49
    NSAIDS, 48
    overview of, 47-48
parasympathetic central nervous system, 1
partial-complex seizure medications, 55
partial-simple seizure medications, 55
passive diffusion, 2
pediatric patients
    ADHD (attention deficit hyperactivity disorder) and, 54-55
    administration to, 2-3
    GERD (gastroesophageal reflux) in, 26-29
    nutritional supplements for, 29
    PNE (primary noctural enuresis) in, 26
    postnatal vs. postconceptual immunization of, 37
    risk for depression, 51
    seizure medications, 55-58
peripheral-acting CNS agents, 13
permethrin-Elimite, Nix, 63
pertussis vaccine, 39
pharmacodynamics, 1
pharmacokinetics, 1
phase one reactions, 4
phase two reactions, 4
phenobarbital, 56-57

phenytoin (Dilantin), 57-58
pinocytosis, 2
PNE (primary nocturnal enuresis), 26
Pneumococcal vaccine, 40
pore transport, 2
postconceptual immunization, 37
postnatal immunization, 37
potassium channel blockers, 11
potassium-sparing diuretics, 24-25
potency, 1
prazosin (Minipress), 13
prednisone, 15-16
Prilosec, 28
Procardia, 11
prokinetics, 28-29
proton pump inhibitors, 28
Proventil, 14-15
Prozac, 51-52
psychiatric drugs
    for ADHD (attention deficit hyperactivity disorder), 54-58
    MAOIs (monoamine oxidase inhibitors), 52-53
    ophthalmologic medications, 58
    overview of, 51
    seizure medications, 55-58
    SSRI (selective serotonin reuptake inhibitors), 51-52
    TCAs (tricyclic antidepressants), 52
Pulmicort, 16
Pulmicort Respules, 16

R

Ranitidine-Zantac, 27-28
reactive airway disease
    anticholinergics for, 16-17
    described, 13-14
    inhaled corticosteroids for, 15-16
    leukotriene modifiers for, 17
    long-acting beta 2 agonists for, 15
    mast cell stabilizers and, 16
    using an MDI (metered dose inhaler) for, 14
    short-acting beta 2 agonists for, 14-15
Reglan, 29-30
Remeron, 53
"rest and digest" response, 1
Retin-A, 63-64
Rocephin, 42-43
route of administration
    absorption following, 2-3
    described, 2
RSV (respiratory syncytial virus) vaccine, 41

S

salmeterol (Serevent), 15

scopolamine (Hyposcine), 2
seizure medications
    carbamazepine (Tegretol), 56
    galapentin (Narontin), 58
    overview of, 55-56
    phenobarbital, 56-57
    phenytoin (Dilantin), 57-58
    valproic acid, valproate (Depakote), 57
Serzone, 53
short-acting beta 2 agonists, 14-15
Singulair, 17
skin lesions
    medications for, 62-64
    overview of, 61-62
sodium channel blockers, 10
spironolactone (Aldactone), 24-25
SSRI (selective serotonin reuptake inhibitors), 51-52
Stevens-Johnson syndrome, 42, 43, 44
Sublimaze, 49-50
SVT (supraventricular tachycardia), 9
synthetic vaccines, 37

T
TCAs (tricyclic antidepressants)
    pain management for, 50
    for pediatric depression, 52
T cell (or cell-mediated immunity), 35
Tegretol, 56
Tenormin, 10
tetanus vaccine, 39
theophylline, 19
theophylline food/drug interactions, 19-20
therapeutic range, 5
thiazide diuretics, 23-24
Thorazine, 53
thyroid medications
    antithyroid drugs, 31-32
    thyroid supplementation, 31
topically administered drugs, 3
toxoids (antigens) vaccine, 37
tretinoin, 63-64
triamcinolone (Azmacort), 15
trimethoprim-Sulfamethoxazole (Cotrim, Bactrim), 41-42
TSH (thyroid regulating hormone), 31
Tylenol, 48-49
type 1 diabetes, 29, 30
type 2 diabetes, 29, 30

V
vaccines
    additional types of, 41
    four types of, 37
    general considerations of, 37-38
    general contraindications of, 38
    Hepatitis B and A, 38-39
    HIB, DTaP, IPV, MMR, 39-40
    immune response and, 35-37
    informed consent prior to administration, 37
    varicella, *pneumococcal, meningitidis,* 40-41
valproic acid, valproate (Depakote), 57
Vanceril, 15
varicella vaccine, 40
Vasotec, 13
Vd (volume of distribution), 4
venlafaxine (Effexor), 53
Ventolin, 14-15
vermox, 43
VRE (vancomycin-resistant enterocci), 37

W
WBC (white blood count), 36
WPW (Wolf-Parkinson-White), 9

X
Xylocaine, 10

Z
Zantac, 27-28
Zestril, 13
Zithromax, 43
Zyvox, 37

PRETEST KEY

Pediatric Pharmacology

1.	b	Chapter 1
2.	a	Chapter 1
3.	b	Chapter 2
4.	d	Chapter 2
5.	a	Chapter 3
6.	a	Chapter 4
7.	b	Chapter 5
8.	a	Chapter 5
9.	c	Chapter 5
10.	c	Chapter 6